D0546667

A Child Called 'IT'

David J. Pelzer

To Chris: My Very Best!! [signature]

OMAHA PRESS PUBLISHING COMPANY, INC.
OMAHA, NEBRASKA

To my son Stephen, who by the grace of God has taught me the gift of love and joy through the eyes of a child.

This book is also dedicated to the teachers and staff of Thomas Edison Elementary School

Steven E. Ziegler
Athena Konstan
Peter Hansen
Joyce Woodworth
Janice Woods
Betty Howell
        and the School Nurse

You put your jobs on the line that fateful March 5, 1973.

You saved my life.

ACKNOWLEDGMENTS

I thank and give credit to all those involved with this project. To my editor Jack Tillman for his skill and his dedication to the integrity of a sensitive subject. To Clint Maun and Raymond Lemke for granting me an interview that cold Christmas Eve and for taking a chance. To my marketing director Sam Tillman for his persistence and patience. To Jack Stovall for holding it all together. To Pat Osborne for a beautiful, powerful cover design. To Anne Hamersky for capturing the photograph of my life. To Kathy Cain and Carol Puffer for their input and technical advice. To Vickie Fisher and Joyce Juracek for their outstanding administrative support. To the entire Maun-Lemke, Inc. staff for their support and encouragement. To Patti Breitman of Breitman Publishing Projects for her initial work and for giving it a good run for the money. To Cindy M. Adams for her unwavering faith when I needed it most. And most important to my wife Phyllis, whom I admire and respect for her endless patience and for never letting me lose faith in the American Dream.

AUTHOR'S NOTES

Some of the names in this book have been changed in order to maintain the dignity and privacy of others.

Chapter 1
The Rescue

M arch 5, 1973, Daly City, California — *I'm late. I just have to finish the dishes on time, otherwise no breakfast; and since I didn't have dinner last night, I have to make sure I get something to eat. My mom's running around yelling at my brothers. I can hear her stomping down the hallway toward the kitchen. I dip my hands back into the scalding rinse water. It's too late. She catches me with my hands out of the water.*

SMACK! She hits me in the face, and I topple to the floor. I know better than to stand there and take the hit. I learned the hard way that she takes that as an act of defiance, which means more hits, or even worse, no food at all. I stand up, dodging her as she screams into my ears.

I act timid, nodding to her threats. "Please," I say to myself, "just let me eat. Hit me again, but I have to have food." Another blow pushes my head against the tile counter top, leaving a bruise I will carry for several days. I let the tears of mock defeat stream down my face. I find that easy to do. She storms out of the kitchen, seemingly satisfied with herself. After I count her steps, making sure she's gone, I breathe a sigh of relief. The act worked again. She can beat me all she wants, but I haven't let her take away my will to find ways to survive.

I finish the dishes and my other chores. My reward is break-fast, which is only leftovers from one of my brothers' cereal bowls. Today it's Lucky Charms. There are only a few bits of cereal left and a half bowl of milk. But as quickly as I can, I swallow it before Mother changes her mind. She has done that before. Once she stood behind me, and a moment before I took a bite of food, she snatched it away and poured it down the garbage disposal. She uses food as a weapon. She knows better than to throw leftovers in the garbage can. She knows I'll dig it out later. She knows most of my tricks.

Now I'm in the old family station wagon, riding through the sunny California spring morning to The Thomas Edison Elementary School like any other kid. I am so late with my chores today that I have to be driven to school. Usually I am forced to run to school. Mother times it so I will arrive just as school begins with no time to steal any food from other kids' lunch boxes.

Mom drops my oldest brother off, but keeps me for a lecture about her plans for me tomorrow. She is going to take me to her brother's house. She says Uncle Dan will TAKE CARE OF ME. She makes it a threat. I give her a frightened look as though I am truly afraid. But I know that even though my uncle is a hard-nosed man, he surely won't treat me like my mom does.

I dash out of the car. Mom yells for me to return. I have forgotten my crumpled lunch bag, which has had the same menu for the last three years – two peanut butter sandwiches and a few carrot sticks. Before I bolt out of the car again, she says, "Tell 'em..., Tell 'em you ran into the door." Then in a voice she rarely uses with me she says, "Have a nice day." I look into her swollen red eyes. She still has a hangover from last night's stupor. Her once beautiful, shiny hair is now frazzled clumps. As usual she wears no make-up. She is overweight, and she knows it which makes it worse. Most of the time this has become her typical appearance.

Because I am so late, I have to report to the Administrative Office. The gray-haired secretary greets me with a smile. Moments later the school nurse comes out and leads me into her office where we go through the normal ritual. First she examines my face and arms. "What's that above your eye?" she asks.

I nod sheepishly, "Oh, I ran into the hall door..., by accident."

Again she smiles and takes a clipboard from the top of a cabinet. She flips through a page or two then bends down to show me. "Here," she points to the paper, "You said that last Monday. Remember?"

I quickly change my story, "I was playing baseball and got hit by the bat. It was an accident." Accident. I am always supposed to say that. But the nurse knows better. She scolds me so I'll tell the truth. I always break down in the end and confess, even though I feel I should protect my mother.

The nurse tells me that I'll be fine and asks me to take off my clothes. We have been doing this since last year so I immediately oblige. My long-sleeve shirt has more holes than Swiss cheese. It's the same shirt I've worn for about two years. Mom has me wear it every day to humiliate me. My pants are just as bad, and my shoes have holes by the toes. I can wiggle my big toe out of one of them. While I stand by clothed only in my underwear, the nurse records my various marks and bruises on the clipboard. She counts the slash-like marks on my face, looking for any she might have missed in the past. She is very thorough. Next the nurse opens my mouth to look at my teeth that are chipped from having been slammed against the kitchen tile counter top. She jots a few more notes on the paper. As she continues to look me over, she stops at the old scar on my stomach. "And that," she says as she takes a deep swallow, "is where she stabbed you?"

"Yes ma'am," I reply. "Oh shit!" I tell myself, "I've done something wrong again." The nurse must see the concern in my eyes. She puts the clipboard down and hugs me. "God," I tell myself, "she is so warm." I don't want to let go. I want to stay in her arms forever. I hold my eyes tightly shut, and for a few moments nothing else exists. She pats my head. I flinch from the sore, swollen bruise Mother gave me this morning. The nurse then breaks the embrace and leaves the room. I rush to put my clothes back on. She doesn't know it, but I do everything as fast as possible.

The nurse returns in a few minutes with Mr. Hansen, the principal, and two of my teachers Miss Woods and Mr. Ziegler. Mr. Hansen knows me very well. I've been in his office more than any other kid in school. He looks at the paper as the nurse reports her findings. He lifts my chin. I'm afraid to look into his eyes, which is mostly a habit from trying to deal with my mom. But it's also because I don't want to tell him anything. Once about a year ago he called Mother to ask about my bruises. At that time he had no idea what was really going on. He just knew I was a troubled kid who was stealing food. When I came to school the next day, he saw the results of Mother's beatings. He never called her again.

Mr. Hansen tells me that he has had enough of this. I almost leap out of my skin. In a panic I begin to explain that I haven't stolen anything today.

Mr. Hansen smiles, "We know that, David. We understand more than you know. In a few minutes we want you to talk to somebody else." Mr. Hansen's smile seems to break the tension and erase the depressed frowns from the faces of the nurse and my teachers. I have no idea that they are all about to risk their jobs to help me.

The Daly City policeman arrives in a few minutes. He first explains why Mr. Hansen has called him. I don't understand everything he says. He wants me to tell him what I have told the others about my mother. I shake my head no. Too many people already know, and I know she will find out. Miss Wood's soft voice calms me. She tells me it is all right. I reluctantly tell them about the beatings, and the nurse has me show the policeman the scar on my stomach. I tell them that the stabbing was an accident, which it was in a way. I also tell them that my mother punishes me because I am bad. I wish they would leave me alone. I know there is nothing anybody can do.

A few minutes later I am excused to sit in the outer office. As I close the door, the adults all look at me and shake their heads in an approving way. I fidget in my chair, watching the secretary type papers. It seems forever before Mr. Hansen calls me back into the room. Miss Woods and Mr. Ziegler leave the lounge. They seem happy, but at the same time worried. Miss Woods kneels down and wraps me in her arms. I don't think I will ever forget the smell of the perfume in her hair. She lets go, turning away so I won't see her cry. Now I am really worried. Mr. Hansen gives me a lunch tray from the cafeteria. "My God! Is it lunch time already?" I ask myself.

I gobble down the food so fast I can hardly taste it. I finish the tray in record time. Soon the principal returns with a box of cookies, warning me not to eat so fast. I have no idea what's going on. One of my guesses is that my father, who is separated from my mother, is coming to get me. But I know that is only a wish. That's not going to happen. The policeman asks for my address and tele-phone number. "That's it!" I tell myself, "It's back to hell. I am going to get it from her again."

The officer writes down more notes as Mr. Hansen and the school nurse look on. Soon he closes his note pad and tells Mr. Hansen that he has enough information. I look up at the principal. He is sweating. I can feel my stomach start to coil. I want to go to the bathroom and throw up.

Mr. Hansen opens the door, and I can see all the teachers on their lunch break staring at me. I am so ashamed. "They know," I tell myself. "They know the truth about my mother, the real truth." It is so important for them to know that I'm not a bad boy. I want so much to be liked, to be loved. I turn down the hall. Mr. Ziegler is holding Miss Woods. She is crying. I can hear her sniffle. She gives me another hug and quickly turns away. Mr. Ziegler shakes my hand. "Be a good boy," he says.

"Yes, sir, I'll try," is all I can say.

The school nurse stands in silence beside Mr. Hansen. They all tell me good-bye. Now I know I am going to jail. "Good," I tell myself. "At least she won't be able to beat me if I'm in jail."

The police officer and I walk outside past the cafeteria. I can see some of the kids from my class playing dodge ball. A few of them stop playing. They yell, "David's busted. David's busted." The policeman touches my shoulder, telling me that everything is O.K. As he drives me up the street away from Thomas Edison Elementary School, I see some kids who seem to be stung by my departure. Before I left, Mr. Ziegler told me he would tell the other kids the truth. I would give anything to have been there in class when they found out I'm not so bad.

In a few minutes we arrive at the Daly City Police Station. I half expect my mother to be there at the station. I don't want to get out of the car. The officer opens the door and gently takes my arm and we walk into a big office. No other person is in the room. The policeman sits in a chair in the corner where he types several sheets of paper. I watch the officer closely and slowly eat my cook-ies. I savor them as long as I can. I don't know when I will be eat-ing again.

It's past one o'clock, and it looks as though the policeman has finished his paperwork. He asks again for my telephone number.

"Why?" I ask.

"I have to call her, David," he says gently.

I want to believe him, but my fear is too great. "No!" I cry, "Send me back to school. You can't let her find out. Don't you understand?"

He calms me down with another cookie as he slowly dials 7-5-6-2-4-6-0. I watch the black dial turn as I get up and walk toward him, straining my whole body trying to hear the phone ringing on the other end. Mom answers. Her voice scares me. The policeman waves me away, and takes a deep breath before saying, "Mrs. Pelzer, this is Officer (I forget his name) from the Daly City Police Department. Your son David will not be coming home today. He will be in the custody of the San Mateo Juvenile Department. If you have any questions, you can call them." He hangs up the phone and smiles, "Now that wasn't so hard, was it?" he asks me. But the look on his face tells me he is assuring himself as much as he is me. I feel my whole life changing.

We are back on highway 280, heading toward the outskirts of Daly City. I look to my right and see a sign that reads, "THE MOST BEAUTIFUL HIGHWAY IN THE WORLD." I am not at all sure about that. The officer smiles with relief as we leave the city limits. "David Pelzer," he says, "you are free."

"What?" I ask, clutching my only source of food. "I don't understand. Aren't you taking me to some kind of jail?"

Again he smiles and gently squeezes my shoulder. "No, David. You have nothing to worry about, honest. Your mother is never going to hurt you again."

I lean back against the seat. A reflection from the sun hits my eyes. I turn away from the rays as a single tear runs down my cheek.

Chapter 2

Good Times

I n the years before I was abused, my family was the "Brady Bunch" of the sixties. My two brothers and I were blessed with what we perceived to be the perfect parents. It seems now that our every whim was fulfilled with love and care.

We lived in a modest two-bedroom house in what was considered a "good" neighborhood in Daly City. I can remember looking out our living room bay window on a clear day to gaze at the bright orange towers of the Golden Gate Bridge and the beautiful skyline of San Francisco.

My father Stephen Joseph supported his family as a fireman working in the heart of San Francisco. He appeared to be everything a child would expect a fireman to be. He stood about five-feet ten-inches tall, and he weighed about one-hundred-ninety pounds. He had broad shoulders and forearms that would make Arnold Schwarzenegger proud. His thick black eyebrows matched his hair. I felt special when he winked at me and called me "Tiger."

I remember my mother, Catherine Roerva, as a woman of average size and appearance. Although I can't recall the color of her hair or eyes, I do remember my childhood feelings. I believe now that at that time in her life she was a woman who glowed with love for her children. Her greatest asset was her determination. She always had ideas, and she always took command of all family matters. She had a way of turning her ideas into action. As I look back now, I see that her ideas might be described better as compulsions. Once when I was four or five years old, Mother said she was sick, and I remember feeling that she did not seem to be herself at all. It

was a day when my father was away from the house working at the
fire station. After serving dinner, she rushed from the table and
began painting the steps that led to the garage. She worked unusu-
ally fast, wiping away the beads of sweat. She also coughed as she
frantically brushed the red paint on the steps. The paint had not
fully dried when she began tacking rubber mats to the steps. The
red paint was all over the mats and Mother. When she finished,
Mother went into the house and collapsed on the couch. I remember asking her, in my childish curiosity, why she had put the mats
down before the paint dried. She smiled and said, "I just wanted to
surprise your dad."

When it came to housekeeping, Mother was an absolute
clean fiend. After feeding my two brothers, Ronald and Stan and
me breakfast, she would dust, disinfect, scour and vacuum. No
room in our house was left untouched. As we grew older, she made
sure we did our part by keeping our room neat. Outside she metic-
ulously attended a small flower garden. She wanted everything she
touched to be perfection. She didn't believe in doing anything
halfway. In those early years Mother often told us that we must
always do the best that we can in whatever we do.

During those early years Mother was truly a gifted cook. Of
all the things she did for her family, I think creating new and exotic
meals was her favorite. This was especially true on those days
when Father was home. Often she would spend the better part of
the day preparing one of her fantastic meals. On some days when
Father was working, she would would take us on exciting sight-
seeing tours around the city. One day the tour was in Chinatown in
San Francisco. As we drove around the area, she told us about the
culture and history of the Chinese people. When we arrived home,
Mother started her record player, and our home was filled with
beautiful sounds from the Orient. She then decorated the dining
room with Chinese lanterns. That evening she dressed in a kimono
and served what to us was a very strange but delicious meal. At the
end of dinner Mother gave us fortune cookies and read the captions
for us. I felt then, as a very young child, that the cookie's message
would lead me to my destiny. Some years later, when I was old
enough to read, I found one of my old fortune cookie messages. It
said, "Love and honor thy mother, for she is the fruit that gives
thou life."

When we were very young, we had a house full of pets including cats, dogs, aquariums filled with exotic fish and a gopher tortoise named "Thor." I remember the tortoise best because Mother let me pick a name for it. I felt proud because my brothers had been chosen to name the other pets and it was now my turn. I named the reptile after my favorite cartoon character.

The five- and ten-gallon aquariums seemed to be everywhere. There were at least two in the living room, and one five-gallon tank filled with guppies was kept in our bedroom. Mother decorated the heated tanks creatively with colored gravel, colored foil backs, anything she thought would make the tanks more realistic. Often we would all sit by the tanks while she told us about the different species of fish.

The most dramatic of Mother's lessons that I can remember came one Sunday afternoon. One of our cats was behaving in an odd way. Mother had us all sit down by the cat while she explained the process of birth. After all the kittens has slipped safely out of the mother cat, she explained in great detail the wonder of life. No matter what the family was doing, she somehow came up with a constructive lesson; often we were not aware that we were being taught.

During those good years, the holidays for our family started with Halloween. One October night when the huge harvest moon was in full view, Mother hurried the three of us out to gaze at the "Great Pumpkin" in the sky. When we returned to our bedroom, she told us to peek under our pillows where we found Matchbox race cars, one of many treasured gifts she provided during the "Brady Bunch" years.

The day after Thanksgiving Mother would dash to the basement and bring up enormous boxes filled with Christmas decorations. Standing on a ladder, she tacked strings of ornaments to the ceiling beams. When she was finished, every room in the house had a seasonal touch. In the dining room she placed various sized red candles on the counter of her cherrywood hutch. Snowflake patterns graced every window in the living room and dining room. Christmas lights were draped around our bedroom windows. Falling asleep while staring at the soft colorful glow of the Christmas lights in the window is still in my memory.

Our Christmas tree was never even an inch under eight feet tall, and it took the whole family hours to decorate it. Each year one of us boys was honored by being allowed to place the angel at the top of the tree while Father held us up in his strong arms. Whoever put the angel on top of the tree felt very important. After the tree was decorated and dinner finished, we would pile into the station wagon and cruise the neighborhood admiring the decorations on other homes. On these trips Mother always talked about her ideas for bigger and better things for the next Christmas. I remember thinking that our house was always the best. When we returned home from looking at other homes, Mother sat us down by the fireplace, and we drank egg nog. While she told us stories, Bing Crosby sang "White Christmas" on the stereo. Often during those holiday seasons I was so excited I couldn't sleep. I recall Mother holding me close while I fell asleep listening to the crackle of the fire.

As Christmas Day came nearer, my brothers and I became more and more enthusiastic. The pile of gifts at the base of the tree seemed to grow day by day. By the time Christmas finally arrived, there were dozens of gifts for each of us.

On Christmas Eve after a special dinner and caroling, we were allowed to open one gift. After that we were sent to bed. Like many children I lay in my bunk bed, straining my ears trying to capture the sound of Santa's sleigh bells. But I always fell asleep before I heard his reindeer land on the roof.

Before dawn Mother would creep into our room and wake us saying, "Santa came!" One year she gave each of us a yellow Tonka plastic hard hat and had us march around the living room. It seemed to take us forever to rip the colorful paper from the boxes to discover what new Christmas delight awaited us. One year she had us run to the back yard in our new robes to look back in through the window at our huge tree. That year, standing in the yard, I remember noticing Mother crying. I asked her if she was sad. She shook her head no, and said she was crying because she was so happy to have a family.

Because Father's job required him to work twenty-four-hour shifts, Mother often took us on day trips to places like the nearby Golden State Park in San Francisco. As we drove slowly through the park, Mother explained how the park's areas were different and how envied the park's flowers were. We always visited the park's Stienhart Aquarium last. My brothers and I would run up the stairs and charge through the heavy doors. We were thrilled as we leaned over the brass sea horse fence looking far below at the small waterfall and pond that was home to the alligators and large turtles. As a child this was my favorite place in the entire park. Once I became frightened as I thought about slipping through the barrier and falling into the pond. Without speaking a word, Mother was sensitive to my fear. She looked down at me and ever so softly held my hand.

Spring meant picnics. Mother would prepare a feast of fried chicken and various salads the night before. Early the next day the family sped off to Junipero Sera Park. Once there my brothers and I ran wild on the grass and pumped higher and higher on the park's swings. Sometimes we would venture off on a new trail. Mother always had to pry us away from our fun when it came time for lunch. We wolfed down our lunch, hardly tasting it, and blitzed off for parts unknown in search of high adventure. Our parents seemed content to lie next to each other on a blanket, sip red wine and watch us play.

It was always a thrill when the family went on summer vacation. Mother was always the driving force behind these trips. She planned every detail and swelled with pride as the activities smoothly came together. Usually we traveled to Portoia or Memorial Park and camped out in our giant green tent for a week or ten days. I shall never forget the thrill of driving over the Golden Gate Bridge as we headed north to the Russian River.

The most memorable trip to the river for me happened the year I was in kindergarten. On the last day of school I was excused a half-hour early as Mother had requested. As Father honked the horn, I rocketed up the small hill from the school to the waiting car. I was excited because I knew where we were going. During the drive I became fascinated at the seemingly endless fields of grapes. When we came into the town of Guerneville, I rolled down my window to smell the sweet air from the pine and redwood trees.

That year a cabin replaced our tent. Each day we enjoyed a new adventure. I remember climbing an old burnt tree stump. Sometimes our parents took us swimming. The river was a whole day's event. We would leave the cabin by nine and return after three. Mother taught us to swim in a small trenched hole in the river. That summer she taught me to swim on my back. She seemed so proud when I was able to do it.

I experienced a magical moment that summer at the river. One day after dinner Mother and Father took the three of us to watch the sunset. The green river water was as smooth as glass. The bluejays scolded the other birds, and a warm breeze blew through my hair. We stood watching the fireball of the sun as it sank behind the tall trees, leaving bright blue and orange streaks in the sky. I felt somebody behind me give me a hug. I thought it was my father. I turned and became flushed with pride to find Mother holding me so tightly. I could feel her heart beat. Never before nor since have I felt quite so safe and warm inside as I did that moment on the river.

Those were perhaps the best times for the whole family. They were surely the best for me. Although I didn't know it then, the "Brady Bunch" era was coming to a close for me. Even as the beatings became commonplace during the later years, whenever we returned to the river we seemed to leave most of the conflict behind. Perhaps that is the reason I still have a deep love for the Russian River in northern California.

Chapter 3
Bad Boy

L ike many forms of child abuse, my case began as discipline
and developed into a kind of life-style that was out of control.
It became so bad at times that I couldn't crawl away, even if it
meant saving my life.

I think the abuse began partly because of my behavior. As a
small boy I probably had a voice that carried farther than some. I
also had the unfortunate luck of getting caught at some covert mis-
chief, even though my brothers and I were often committing the
same "crime." In the beginning I was put in a corner of our bedroom. By this time I had become afraid of Mother. I never asked
her to let me come out. I would sit and wait for one of my brothers
to come into our room and I'd have him ask if David could come
out now and play.

About this time Mother's behavior began to change radically.
At times while Father was away at work, she would spend the
entire day lying on the couch dressed in her bathrobe watching
television. She got up only to go to the bathroom, get another drink
or heat leftover food. When she yelled at us, her voice had changed
from the soothing mother to the Wicked Witch of the North. Soon
the sound of her voice began to send tremors down my spine. Even
when she barked at one of my brothers, I'd run, hiding in our room
hoping she would soon return to the couch, her drink and her TV
show. After a while I could determine what kind of a day I was
going to have by the way she dressed. I would breathe a sigh of
relief whenever I saw her come out of her room in a nice dress
with her face made up. On these days she always came out with a
smile.

When Mother decided that the "corner treatment" was no longer effective, I graduated to the "mirror treatment." In the beginning it was a no-notice form of punishment. It came suddenly when I least expected it. Mother would simply grab me and smash my face against the mirror, smearing my tear-streaked face on the slick, reflective glass. Then she would order me to say over and over again, "I am a bad boy! I am a bad boy! I am a bad boy!" I was then left to stand there, staring into the mirror. I would stand there until I ached, dreading the moment when the second set of commercials aired stopping one of Mother's television shows. I knew she would soon be stomping down the hall to see if my face was still against the mirror and to tell me what a sickening child I was. Whenever my brothers came into the room while I was at the mirror, they would look at me, shrug their shoulders and continue to play as if I were not there. At first I was jealous, but soon I learned that they were only trying to save their own skins.

Often while Father was at work, Mother would yell and scream while forcing us to search the entire house for something she had lost. The quest usually started in the morning and lasted for hours. After a while I was usually sent to search in the garage which was under part of the house like a basement. Even there I trembled upon hearing her scream at one of my brothers.

The fruitless searches continued for months, and finally I was the only one singled out to look for her things. Once I forgot what I was looking for. When I timidly asked her what it was that I was to find, she smacked me in the face. She was lying on the couch at the time, and she didn't even stop watching her television show. Blood gushed from my nose and I began to cry. Mother snatched a napkin from her table, tore off a piece and rammed it up my nose. "You know damn well what you are looking for!" she screamed. "Now go find it!" I scurried down to the basement, making sure I made enough noise to convince her that I was feverishly obeying her command. After few more similar incidents, I began to fantasize that I had found her article. I would imagine myself marching upstairs with my prize and Mother greeting me with hugs and kisses. My fantasy included the family living happily ever after. In reality I never found any of Mother's lost things, and she never let me forget that I was an incompetent loser.

In the early days of the abuse Mother was as different as

night and day when Father was home from work. She fixed her hair and put on nice clothes and she seemed more relaxed. I loved it when Dad was home. It meant no beatings, mirror treatments or long searches for her missing things. I came to believe that Father was my protector. Whenever he went to the garage to work on a project, I followed him. If he sat in his favorite chair to read the newspaper, I parked myself at his feet. In the evenings after the dinner dishes were cleared from the table, Father would wash and I would dry them. I knew that as long as I stayed by his side, no harm would come to me.

One day before he left for work, I received a dreadful shock. After he said goodbye to Ron and Stan, he knelt down, held my shoulders tightly and told me to be a "good boy." Mother stood behind him with her arms folded across her chest and a smile on her face that seemed cold rather than warm. I looked into my father's eyes and knew right then that I was a bad boy. An ice-cold chill rushed through my body. I wanted to hold on to him and never let go but before I could give him a hug, he stood up, turned and walked out the door without saying another word.

For a short time after Father's warning, things seemed to calm down between Mother and me. When Dad was home, my brothers and I played in our room or outside until about three in the afternoon. Mother would then turn on the television so we could watch cartoons. For my parents three o'clock had become the "Happy Hour." Father would cover the kitchen counter top with bottles of alcohol and tall fancy glasses. He cut up lemons and limes, placing them in small bowls beside a small jar of cherries. They often drank from mid-afternoon until my brothers and I climbed into bed. I remember watching them dance around the kitchen to music from the radio. They held each other close, and they looked so happy. At those times I thought I could bury the bad times. I was wrong. The bad times were only beginning.

A month or two later on a Sunday while Father was at work, my brothers and I were playing in our room when we heard Mother rush down the hall yelling at us. Ron and Stan ran for cover in the living room. I instantly sat down in my chair. With both arms stretched out and raised she came at me. As she came closer and closer, I backed my chair toward the wall. Soon my head touched the wall. Mother's eyes were glazed and red, and her breath smelled of booze. I closed my eyes as the oncoming blows began to rock me from side to side. I tried to protect my face with my hands, but Mother only knocked them away. Her punches seemed to last forever. Finally I worked my left arm up to cover my face. As she grabbed my arm, she lost her balance and staggered back a step. As she jerked violently to regain her stability, I heard something pop and felt an intense pain in my shoulder and arm. The startled look on her face told me that she had heard the sound too, but she released her grip on my arm and turned and walked away as if nothing had happened. I cradled my arm as it began to throb with pain. Before I could actually inspect my arm, Mother summoned me to dinner.

I dutifully sat down at a T.V. tray to try and eat. As I reached for a glass of milk, my left arm did not respond. My fingers twitched upon command, but my arm tingled and had become lifeless. I looked at Mother, trying to plead with my eyes, but she ignored me. Although I knew something was very wrong, I was afraid to say anything. I simply sat there, staring at my tray of food. Mother finally excused me and sent me to bed early telling me to sleep in the top bunk. This was unusual because I always slept on the bottom. Sometime near morning I finally fell asleep with my left arm carefully cradled in the other.

I hadn't slept long when Mother awakened me explaining that I had rolled out of the top bunk during the night. She appeared to be deeply concerned about my well-being as she drove me to the hospital. When she told the doctor about my fall from the top bunk bed, I could tell by the look he gave me that he knew the injury was no accident. I was too afraid to say anything. At home Mother made up an even more colorful story for Father. In the new version she included her efforts to save me before I hit the floor. As I sat in her lap listening to her lie to Father, I knew in my child's mind that something was seriously wrong with her. My fear kept the incident Mother's and my secret, for I knew if I said anything the next "accident" might be worse.

At first school was a haven for me. It helped so much to get away from Mother. At recess I was a wild man. I played in the tan bark-covered area of the playground, looking for new adventurous things to do. I made friends easily and felt happy at school. One day in late spring when I returned home from school, Mother threw me bodily into her room. She then yelled at me saying that I was to be held back from the first grade because I was a bad boy. I was bewildered. I knew I had more "happy face" papers than anybody in the class. I knew I obeyed my teacher and that she liked me. But Mother continued to roar that I had shamed the family and would be severely punished. She decided that I was banned from watching television. I was to go without dinner and accomplish whatever chores she could create. After another thrashing I was sent to the garage to stand until she called me to go to bed.

That summer when the family went camping I received one of the most devastating blows of my life. Without warning I was dropped off at my Aunt Jose's house on the way to the campsite. I felt like an outcast as the station wagon drove away leaving me behind. I was so sad at this turn of events that in a few days I tried to run away from my aunt's house. I wanted to find my family, and for some strange reason I wanted to be with my mother. Of course, I didn't get far, and later my aunt informed my mother of my attempt to run away. Mother didn't say anything at first, but the next time my father worked the twenty-four-hour shift I paid for my sin. Mother smacked, punched and kicked me until I crumpled to the floor. I tried to tell her that I had run away because I wanted to be with her and the family. I tried to tell her that I had missed her, but she refused to let me speak. I tried once more and Mother dashed to the bathroom, snatched a bar of soap and crammed it down my throat. After that I was no longer allowed to speak unless I was told to do so.

Returning to the first grade was really a joy. I knew the basic lessons and was almost instantly dubbed the class genius. My retention had placed Stan and me in the same grade. During recess I would go over to Stan's first-grade class to play. At school we were inseparable; however, at home we both knew I was not to be acknowledged.

One day I rushed home to show off a school paper. Mother threw me into her bedroom yelling she had received a letter from the North Pole. She claimed the letter said that I was a bad boy and Santa would not bring me any gifts for Christmas. She raged on and on saying that again I had embarrassed the family. I stood in a daze as Mother badgered me relentlessly. I felt I was living in a nightmare that Mother had created, and I prayed she would wake up. Before Christmas that year there were only a couple of gifts for me under the tree, and those came from relatives outside the immediate family. On Christmas morning Stan asked Mother why Santa had brought me only two paint-by-number pictures. She lectured him stating, "Santa only brings toys to good boys and girls." I stole a glance at Stan. There was sorrow in his eyes, and I could tell that he understood Mother's freakish games. Since I was still under punishment, on Christmas Day I had to change into my work clothes and complete some chores. While I was cleaning the bathroom, I overheard an argument between Mother and Father. She was angry with him for "going behind (her) back" to buy me the paintings. Mother told Father that she was in charge of disciplining "the boy" and that he had undermined her authority by buying the gifts. The longer Father argued his case, the angrier she became. I could tell he had lost his case and that I was becoming more and more alone.

A few months later my mother became a den-mother for the Cub Scouts. Whenever the other kids came to our home, she treated them like kings. Some of the other kids told me how they wished their mothers would be like mine. I said little when they made these kinds of statements, but I wondered to myself what they would think if they knew the truth. Mother kept the den-mother job for only a few months. When she gave it up, I was relieved because it meant I could go to the home of some other kid for the Wednesday meetings.

One Wednesday I came home from school to change into my blue and gold Cub Scout uniform. Mother and I were the only ones in the house, and I could tell by the look on her face that she was after blood. After smashing my face against the bedroom mirror, she dragged me out to the car. During the drive to my den-mother's house, Mother told me what she was going to do with me when we got home. I scooted to the far side of the front seat of the car, but it didn't work. She reached across the seat and seized my chin and jaw, lifting my head toward hers. Her eyes were bloodshot and her voice sounded as if she were possessed. When we arrived at the den-mother's house, I ran to the door crying and told the den mother that I had been a bad boy and could not attend the meeting. She smiled politely saying that she would like me to come to the next meeting. That was the last time I saw her.

Once home Mother ordered me to strip off my clothes and stand by the kitchen stove. I shook from a combination of fear and embarrassment. She then revealed my hideous crime. Mother told me that she had often driven to school to watch my brothers and me play during our lunch period recess. She said that she had that very day seen me playing on the grass which was forbidden by her rules. I protested truthfully that I had never broken the rules by playing on the grass. I told her that she had somehow made a mistake. My reward for observing her rules and telling the truth was a hard punch in the face.

Mother then reached up and turned on the gas burners on the kitchen stove. She told me that she had read an article about a mother who had her son lie on top of a hot stove. I was terrified. My brain became numb, and my legs wobbled like jelly. I wanted to disappear. I closed my eyes, wishing her away. I felt her hand clamp my arm as if it were in a vice grip.

"You have made my life a living hell!" she sneered. "Now it is time I showed you what hell is like." Holding my arm tightly, Mother pushed it toward the orange-blue flame. My skin seemed to explode from the heat, and I could smell the scorched hairs from my burnt arm. This time I fought back. My panic seemed to make me stronger, and I was able to force her to release her grip on my arm. I fell to the floor on my hands and knees and began to blow cool air on the red spot on my arm. "It's too bad your drunken father is not here to save you," she hissed. Mother then ordered me to climb up onto the stove and lie on the flames so she could watch me burn. I refused, crying and pleading. I felt my own rage give me strength, and I stomped my feet in protest. But she continued to try to get me on top of the stove. I watched the flames, praying the gas might run out.

Suddenly I began to realize that the longer I could keep myself off the top of the stove, the better my chances were. I knew my brother Ron would soon be coming home from his scout meeting, and I knew she wouldn't continue to try to put me on the stove when he was in the house. As I struggled, I watched the clock. The second hand seemed to move ever so slowly. To keep her further off balance, I began to ask whining questions. This infuriated her even more, and she began to rain blows around my face and head. When Mother began to hit me, I knew I had won. The blows hurt, but I knew they were better than getting on top of the flaming stove.

Finally, I heard the front door open. It was Ron. My heart surged with relief. The look on Mother's face told me that this time she knew she had lost. She backed away, and I seized that instant to grab my clothes and race to the garage where I quickly dressed. I stood against the wall and began to whimper until I realized that I had beaten her. I had bought a few precious minutes. I had used my head to survive. For the first time, I had won!

The decision I made the day of the stove incident was perhaps the most important decision of my life. Standing alone in that damp, dark garage, I knew for the first time that I could survive. I decided that I would use any tactic I could think of to defeat Mother or to delay her from her grizzly obsession. I knew I would have to think ahead. I could no longer cry like a helpless baby. In order to survive, I could never give in to her. That day I vowed to myself to never again give that bitch the satisfaction of hearing me beg her to stop beating me.

I will never forget how cold it was in the garage on the day of the stove incident. My entire body trembled from both the cold and my fear. I used my tongue to lick the burn on my throbbing arm. I wanted to scream, but I was resolved not to give Mother the pleasure of hearing me cry. I stood tall. I could hear Mother talking to Ron upstairs. She was telling him how proud she was of him and how she didn't have to worry about him becoming like David, a bad boy.

Chapter 4

The Fight For Food

I became anxious for school to start. Except for the short dura-
tion of a fishing trip, things with Mother were touch and go,
or perhaps better described as smash and dash. She would smash
me, and I would dash to the solitude of the basement. Actually the
basement and the garage were the same thing. The garage was
under part of the house so we sometimes called it the basement.
The month of September brought school and bliss. I had new
clothes and a shiny new lunch pail. However, by October my
clothes had become weathered and torn. Mother made me wear the
same thing week after week. I often went to class with bruises on
my face and arms. It was also common practice for me to go to bed
without dinner. Breakfast wasn't much better. It was just left-over
cereal portions from my brothers, and only if I finished certain
chores before going to school.

At night I was so hungry my stomach growled as if I were an
angry bear. At night I lay awake thinking of food. "Maybe tomorrow I will get dinner," I said to myself. After what seemed like
hours, I would drift off to sleep. More than once I dreamt about
food. The subject of many of my dreams was a colossal hamburger
with all the fixings. In the dreams I seized the prize and brought it
to my lips. I visualized every inch of the hamburger. The meat
dripped with grease, and thick slices of cheese bubbled on top.
Condiments oozed between the lettuce and tomato. The dream was
as cruel as Mother. As I brought the dream hamburger closer to my
face, I opened my mouth to devour my prize, but nothing happened. I tried again and again, but the dream was elusive and I
experienced no taste no matter how hard I concentrated. Moments

later I would wake up, my stomach more hollow than before. I could not satisfy my hunger; not even in my dreams.

Soon after I had begun to dream about food, I started stealing food at school. My stomach coiled with a combination of fear and anticipation. Anticipation because I knew that within seconds I would have something to put in my stomach. Fear because I also knew that at any time I could get caught stealing the food. I always stole food before school began while my classmates were playing outside the building. I would sneak to the wall right outside my home room, drop my lunch pail by another pail and kneel down so nobody could see me rummaging through other students' lunches. The first few times were easy, but after a few days other students began to discover Twinkies and other desserts missing from their lunches. Within a short time I was discovered, and my peers began to detest me. The teacher informed the principal who in turn informed Mother. The cycle became a full circle. The principal's report to Mother led to more beatings and less food for me at home, a condition which drove me to more stealing to satisfy my great hunger. She even withheld food during weekends. I suffered more then because I could not get out to steal any food.

By Sunday night, my mouth would actually water, and I would plot new, surer ways to steal food without getting caught. One of my plots was to steal from different first-grade rooms where I wasn't known as well. On Monday mornings I would dash from Mother's car to a new first-grade classroom to pick through lunch boxes. This method was successful for a short time, but it didn't take the principal long to trace the thefts back to me.

At home the dual punishment of hunger and violent attacks continued. By this time for all practical purposes, I was no longer a member of the family. I existed, but there was little or no recognition. Mother had even stopped using my name, referring to me only as "the boy." I was not allowed to eat meals with the family. I was not allowed to play with my brothers. I was not allowed to watch television. I was grounded to the house. I was not allowed to look at or speak to anybody. When I returned home from school, I immediately accomplished the various chores Mother had assigned me. When the chores were finished, I went directly to the basement where I stood until summoned to clear the dinner table and wash the dishes. It was made very clear that getting caught sitting or lying down in the basement would bring dire consequences. I had become a slave.

Father was my only hope, and I think that at times he did all he could to get me some food. At times he tried to get Mother drunk, thinking that the liquor might leave her in a better mood. He tried to get her to change her mind about feeding me. He tried to make deals, promising her the world. But all his attempts were futile. Mother was as solid as a rock. If anything, her drunkenness made it worse. She became more like a monster.

Father's attempts to help me finally led to stress between him and Mother and midnight arguments began to occur. From my bed I could hear the tempo build to an ear-shattering climax. By then they were both drunk, and I could hear Mother scream every vulgar phrase imaginable. It didn't matter what issue started the fight, I would soon be the object of the battle. I knew Father was trying to help, but in my bed I shivered with fear. I knew he would lose, making things worse for me the next day. When they first began to fight, Mother would drive off in the car with the tires screeching. She usually returned home in less than an hour. The next day they would both act as if nothing had happened. I was grateful when Father found an excuse to come down the basement and sneak me a piece of bread. He always promised me he would try again.

As the arguments between Mother and Father became more frequent, he began to change. Often after an argument he would pack an overnight bag and set off in the middle of the night for work. After he had gone, Mother would yank me out of bed and drag me to the kitchen. While I stood shivering in my pajamas she smacked me from one side of the kitchen to the other. One of my resistance techniques was to lay on the floor acting as though I didn't have the strength to stand. This technique didn't last long. Mother would pick me up by the ears and yell into my face with her bourbon breath for minutes at a time. On these nights her message was always the same: I was the reason she and Father were having problems. Often I became so tired my legs would shake. My only escape was to stare at the floor and hope that Mother would run out of steam.

By this time I was in the second grade and Mother was pregnant with her fourth child. My teacher that year was Miss Moss and she took a special interest in me. She began by questioning me about my attentiveness. I lied saying that I had stayed up late watching television. My lies were not convincing, however, and she continued to question me not only about why I was sleepy but also about the condition of my clothes and the bruises on my arms. Mother had always coached me about what to say about the marks on my face and I simply passed her story along to the teacher.

Months crept by and Miss Moss became less and less satisfied with my answers. One day she finally reported her concerns to the school principal. He knew me well as the food thief, so he called Mother. When I went home that day, it was as if somebody had dropped an atomic bomb. Mother was more violent than ever. She was furious that some "Hippie" teacher had turned her in for child abuse. She said that she would meet with the principal on the very next day to account for all the false accusations. By the end of the session my nose had bled twice and I was missing a tooth.

When I returned from school the next day, Mother smiled as if she had won a million-dollar sweepstakes. She told me how she had dressed up and gone to see the principal with my infant brother Russell in her arms. She told me how she had explained to the principal how David had an overactive imagination. Mother told him how David had often struck and scratched himself to get attention since the recent birth of his new brother Russell. I could imagine her turning on her snake-like charm as she cuddled Russell for the benefit of the principal. At the end of their talk Mother said that she was more than happy to cooperate with the school. She said they could call her any time there was a problem with David. She was sure she could help them. When she talked to the school it was "David" not "the boy." As Mother told me about the meeting I could sense her heightened confidence, and her new confidence made me fear for my life. Mother said the staff at school had been instructed to pay no attention to my wild stories of child beating or not being fed. Standing there in the kitchen that day listening to her boast gave me a complete feeling of emptiness. I wished in my childish way that I could dissolve and be gone forever. I wished I would never have to face another human being again.

That summer the family vacationed at the Russian River. Although I got along better with Mother, the magical feeling had disappeared. The hayrack rides, the weenie roasts and story telling were a thing of the past. We spent more and more time in the cabin. Even the day trips to the river were rare.

Father tried to make the vacation more fun by taking the three of us to play on the giant new slide. Russell, who was still a toddler, stayed home with Mother. One day when Ron, Stan and I were playing at a neighbor's cabin, Mother came out onto the porch and yelled for us to come in immediately. Once in the cabin I was scolded for making too much noise. For my punishment I was not allowed to go with Father and my brothers to the super slide. I sat in a corner on a chair shivering, hoping that something would happen so the three of them wouldn't leave. I knew Mother had something hideous on her mind. As soon as they left, she brought out one of Russell's soiled diapers. She smeared the diaper on my face. I tried to sit perfectly still. I knew if I moved, it would only be worse. I didn't look up. I couldn't see Mother standing over me, but I could hear her heavy breathing.

After what seemed like an hour, Mother knelt down beside me and in a soft voice said, "Eat it".

I looked straight ahead, avoiding her eyes. "No way!" I said to myself. Like so many times before, it was the wrong thing to do. As if she knew my feelings, Mother smacked me from side to side. I clung to the chair, fearing that if I fell off, she would jump on me.

"I said eat it!" she sneered.

Switching tactics, I began to cry. "Slow her down," I thought to myself. I began to count to myself, trying to concentrate. Like many times before my only ally was time. Mother answered my crying with more blows to my face and stopped only when she heard Russell crying.

Even with my face covered with defecation, I was pleased. I thought I might win. I tried to wipe the shit away, flicking it onto the wooden floor. I could hear Mother singing softly to Russell, and I imagined him cradled in her arms. I prayed he wouldn't fall asleep. A few minutes later my luck ran out.

Still smiling, Mother returned to her conquest. She grabbed me by the back of the neck and led me to the kitchen. There, spread out on the counter top, was another full diaper. The smell turned my stomach. "Now you are going to eat it!" she said. Mother had the same look in her eyes that she had the day she wanted me to lie on top of the gas stove back home. Without moving my head, I moved my eyes searching for the daisy-colored clock that I knew was on the wall. It was a few seconds before I realized that the clock was behind me. Without the clock I felt helpless. I knew that I needed to lock my concentration on something in order to keep any kind of control of my mind. Before I could find the clock, Mother's hands seized my neck. Again she repeated, "Eat it!" I held my breath. The smell was overpowering. I tried to concentrate on the top corner of the diaper. Seconds seemed like hours. Mother most have known my plan. She slammed my face into the diaper and rubbed it from side to side.

I anticipated her move and as I felt my head being forced down, I closed my eyes tightly and clamped my mouth shut. My nose struck first. A warm sensation oozed from my nostrils. I tried to stop the blood from escaping by breathing in. When I did this, I snorted bits of defecation back up my nose with the blood. I threw my hands on the counter top and tried to pry myself out of her grip. I twisted from side to side with all my strength, but she was too powerful. Suddenly Mother let go. "They're back! They're back!" she gasped. She had as little breath left as I did. Mother quickly grabbed a wash cloth from the sink and threw it at me. "Clean the shit off your face," she said as she wiped the brown stains from the counter top. I wiped my face the best I could, but not before blowing bits of defecation from my nose. Moments later Mother stuffed a piece of cloth up my bloody nose and ordered me to sit in the corner. I sat there for a long time, still smelling traces of my experience in my nose.

The family never returned to the Russian River again.

In September I returned to school with no new clothes and my old, rusted, green lunch pail. My clothes were a disgrace. Mother packed the same lunch for me every day: two peanut butter sandwiches and a few limp carrot sticks. Since I was no longer a member of the family, I was not allowed to ride to school in the family station wagon. Mother had me run to school. She knew I would not arrive in time to steal any food from my classmates.

At school I was a total outcast. No other kid would have anything to do with me. During the lunch recesses I stuffed the sandwiches down my throat as I listened to my former friends make up songs about me. "David the Food Thief" and "David the Smelly Bum" are two I remember. I had no one to talk to or play with. I felt all alone.

I knew that I wouldn't make it on the meager lunch Mother was providing for me. At home while standing for hours in the garage, I passed the time by imagining new ways to steal food. Father was still trying to sneak scraps of food to me, but he had little success. I had come to the conclusion that if I were to survive, I would have to rely on myself. I had exhausted all possibilities at school. All the students now hid their lunch pails. The teachers and principal knew me and watched me. I had very little chance of stealing any more food at school.

Finally I devised a plan that might work. Students were not allowed to leave the playground during lunch recess, so nobody would expect me to leave. My idea was to sneak away from the playground and run to the local grocery store and steal cookies, bread, chips or whatever I could. In my mind I carefully planned every step of my scheme. When I ran to school in the morning, I counted every step so I could calculate my pace and apply it later to my trip to the store. After a few weeks I had all the information I needed. All that was left then was finding the courage to try the plan. I knew it would take longer to go from the school to the store because it was up a hill, so I allowed fifteen minutes. Coming back downhill would be easier, so I allowed ten minutes. This plan provided ten minutes to do my business at the store.

Each day when I ran to and from school, I tried to run faster, pounding each step as if I were a marathon runner. As the days passed and my plan became more solid, I replaced my hunger for food with daydreaming. I used this technique while doing my chores at home. On my hands and knees scrubbing the bathroom tile, I imagined I was the Prince in the story "The Prince and the Pauper." As the Prince I knew I could end the charade of acting like a servant any time I wanted. In the basement I stood erect with my eyes closed, dreaming I was a comic-book character. I waited for a far-away crisis to erupt so I could rush in and save the "good people" and become everybody's hero. But the daydream was always interrupted by hunger pangs, and my thoughts returned to my plan for stealing food.

Even when I was sure my plan was foolproof, I was afraid to put it into action. During the lunch recess at school I strolled around the play yard making excuses to myself for my inability to put my plan into action. I told myself I would get caught or that my timing calculations were not accurate. All through the argument with myself, my stomach growled, calling me "chicken." Finally, after several days without dinner and only the small left-over portions for breakfast, I decided to do it. A few moments after the lunch bell had rung, I blitzed up the street away from the school with my heart pounding and my lungs bursting for air. I made it to the store in half the time I had allotted myself. Walking up and down the aisles of the store, I felt as if everybody was staring at me. I felt as though all the customers were talking about the smelly, ragged child. I felt that my plan was doomed because I hadn't taken into account how I might look to other people. The more I worried about how conspicuous I was, the more my stomach was seized with fear. I became frozen in the aisle not knowing what to do. I slowly began to count the seconds away. Slowly, between the numbers, I began to think about all the time I had been so hungry. This seemed to calm me, and without thinking about the consequences, I grabbed the first thing I saw on the shelf, ran out of the store and raced back to school. Clutched tightly in my hand was a small box of graham crackers.

As I came near the school I hid my prize under my shirt on the side that didn't have any holes and tried to be calm as I walked through the doors. Inside I ditched the food in the trash can in the boys' rest room. Later in the afternoon after making some excuse to the teacher, I returned to the rest room to devour my prize. My heart sank as I looked into the empty trash can. All my careful plans and all the pain of convincing myself that I would eat were wasted. The custodian had emptied the trash can before I got back to the rest room.

My store plan failed the first day, but on other occasions it succeeded. Once I managed to hide my treasure in my desk in my home room only to find on the next day that I had been transferred to the school across the street. Except for losing the stolen food, I welcomed the transfer. At the new school I felt I had a new license to steal. And for a while I was able to steal from my classmates again, but I also sprinted to the store about once a week. Sometimes, if things weren't just right, I didn't steal anything. But often I did, and as I should have expected, I finally got caught. The manager called Mother. At home I was thrashed relentlessly.

Mother knew why I was stealing and so did Dad, but she continued to refuse to feed me. The more I craved food, the more I tried to come up with a better plan.

It was Mother's habit to scrape the leftovers from the dinner plates into a small garbage can under the sink. After this was done, she would summon me up from the basement where I had been standing while the family ate. It was my job to wash the dishes. Standing there with my hands in the scalding water, I could smell the scraps from dinner in the small garbage can. At first the idea was nauseating, but the more I thought about it, the better it seemed. It was my only hope for food. I finished the dishes as fast as I could and emptied the garbage myself in the garage. My mouth watered at the sight of the food, and I gingerly picked good pieces out and scraped bits of paper or cigarette butts away and ate it as fast as I could.

As usual my new plan came to an abrupt halt when Mother caught me in the act. For a few weeks I quit the garbage plan, but I finally had to return to it in order to silence my growling stomach. Once I ate some left-over pork that was so bad I had diarrhea for a week. While I was sick, Mother told me that she had purposefully left the meat in the refrigerator for two weeks to spoil before she threw it away. She knew I couldn't resist stealing it. As time progressed, Mother had me bring the garbage can to her so she could inspect it while she lay on the couch. She never discovered that often I would wrap food between paper towels and hide them in the bottom of the can. I knew she wouldn't want to get her fingers dirty digging in the bottom of the trash can, so my scheme worked for a while.

Mother knew I was getting food some way, so she began sprinkling ammonia in the trash can. After that I gave up on the garbage at home and set my sights on finding some way to get food at school. I knew that my string had run out stealing from other kids' lunches. My next idea was stealing frozen lunches from the school cafeteria.

I timed my rest room break so the teacher excused me from the classroom just after the truck carrying the frozen lunches dropped off its supplies. I knew that there were no cooks in the kitchen at that time. I crept into the cafeteria and snatched some frozen trays and scurried to the rest room. In the solitude of the rest room I bit the frozen hot dogs and tater tots into huge chunks and swallowed them, almost choking myself in the process. Minutes later I returned to my classroom feeling proud of myself. I was sure I had beaten Mother and her attempts to starve me.

As I ran home from school on the day I stole the frozen food, all I could think about was what I might be able to steal from the cafeteria on the next day. When I arrived at Mother's house, she changed my mind. She dragged me into the bathroom and hit me in the stomach so hard that I bent over. Pulling me around to face the toilet, she ordered me to shove my finger down my throat. At first I resisted. I tried my old trick of counting to myself as I stared into the porcelain toilet bowl, "One..two.." I never made it to three. Mother rammed her finger into my mouth as if she wanted to pull my stomach up through my throat. I squirmed in every direction in an effort to fight her. She finally let me go, but only when I agreed that I would vomit for her.

I knew what was going to happen even before I shoved my finger in my mouth. I closed my eyes as chunks of red meat spilled into the toilet. Mother just stood behind me with her hands on her hips and said, "I thought so. Your Father is going to hear about this!" I tensed myself for the volley of blows that I knew was on the way. When nothing happened after a few seconds, I turned around to discover that Mother had left the bathroom. I knew, however, that the episode wasn't over. She soon returned with a small bowl and had me scoop the partially digested food out of the toilet and put it in the bowl. Father was away from the house shopping at the time, and she was gathering evidence for his return.

Later that night after I finished all of my evening chores, Mother had me stand by the kitchen table while she and Father talked in the bedroom. In front of me was the bowl of hot dogs that I had vomited. I couldn't look at it, so I closed my eyes and tried to imagine that I was some other place. After a while I heard my parents enter the kitchen. "Look at this, Steve," Mother barked, thrusting her finger in the direction of the bowl. "So you think the boy is through stealing food, do you?"

By the look on Father's face, I could tell he was getting more and more tired of the constant "What has 'the boy' done now" routine." Staring at me he shook his head in disapproval and said sadly, "Well, Roerva, if you would just let the boy have some food."

A heated battle of words broke out in front of me, and as always, Mother won. "EAT! You want the boy to eat, Stephen? Well, he is going to EAT! He is going to eat this!" Mother yelled at the top of her voice, pushing the bowl toward me and stomping off to the bedroom.

The kitchen suddenly became very quiet. So quiet I could hear Father's uneven breathing. He gently placed his hand on my shoulder and said, "Wait here, Tiger, I'll see what I can do." He returned a few minutes later after trying to talk Mother out of her demand. By the saddened look on his face, I knew immediately who had won.

I sat on a chair and picked the clumps of the hot dogs out of the bowl with my hand. Blobs of thick saliva slipped through my fingers as I dropped it in my mouth. As I tried to swallow, I began to whimper. I turned to Father, who stood there looking at me with a drink in his hand. He nodded for me to continue. I couldn't believe he was just standing there as I ate the revolting contents of the bowl. I knew for sure that we were slipping farther and farther apart. So far apart that it would soon be forever.

I tried to swallow without chewing until I felt a hand clamp on the back of my neck. "Chew it!" Mother snarled, "Eat it! Eat it all!" she said, pointing to the saliva. I sat deeper in my chair. A river of tears rolled down my cheeks. After I had chewed the miserable mess in the bowl, I tilted my head back and forced what remained down my throat. I closed my eyes and screamed to myself to keep it from coming back up into my mouth. I didn't open my eyes until I was sure my stomach wasn't going to reject the slimy hot dogs. When I did open them, I looked at Father. He only turned away without looking at me. At that moment I hated Mother to no end, but I hated Father more. The man who had helped me in the past just stood by quietly while his son ate something even a dog wouldn't touch.

Soon after I finished the bowl of regurgitated hot dogs, Mother returned in her robe and threw a wad of newspapers at me. She told me that the papers were my blankets and the floor under the table was my bed. Again I shot a glance at Father, but he acted as though I was not even in the room. I crawled fully dressed under the table, covering myself with the newspapers like a rat in a cage.

For months I slept under the breakfast table next to a box of kitty litter. I soon learned to use the newspapers to my advantage. With the papers wrapped around me, my body heat kept me warm. Finally Mother told me that I was no longer privileged enough to sleep upstairs, and I was banished downstairs to the garage and an old army cot. To stay warm, I tried to keep my head close to the gas heater. But after a few cold nights I found it best to keep my hands clamped under my arms and my feet curled toward my buttocks. Sometimes at night I would awake and try to imagine that I was one of my brothers sleeping under a warm electric blanket, knowing I was safe and knowing that somebody cared for me. This worked for a while, but the cold always brought me to the reality of my situation. I felt that no one could help me. Not my teachers, the staff at school, my brothers or even my father. I was on my own, and every night I prayed to God that I could be strong both in body and soul. So in the darkness of the cold night, I lay on the wooden cot and shivered until I fell into a restless sleep.

Once during my midnight fantasies, I came up with the idea of begging food on my way to school. Even though the after-school vomit inspection was carried out every day when I came home from school, I thought that any food I ate in the morning would be digested by then. As I began my run to school, I made sure I ran extra fast so I would have more time for my quest for food. I then altered my course, stopping and knocking on doors. I would ask the lady who answered my knock if she had happened to find a lunch box near her house. For the most part my plan worked. I could tell by looking at them that the ladies who gave me lunch felt sorry for me. I used a fake name so nobody would know who I was. This worked until the day I came to the house of a lady who knew Mother. My time-tested story, "I lost my lunch; could you make me one?" fell apart. I knew she would call Mother.

All that day at school I prayed for the world to come to an end. As I sat in the classroom, I knew Mother was watching television and getting drunker by the hour, while she thought of something hideous to do to me when I arrived at "her" home after school. Running home from school that afternoon, my feet felt as though they were encased in blocks of cement. With every step I prayed that Mother's friend had not called her or had somehow mistaken me for another child. Above me the skies were blue, and I could feel the sun's rays warm my back. As I approached Mother's house, I looked up toward the sun, really wondering if I would ever see it again. I opened the front door and tiptoed down the stairs to the garage. I expected Mother to fly down the stairs and beat me on the cement floor any second, but she didn't come. After changing into my work clothes, I proceeded upstairs to the kitchen and began washing Mother's lunch dishes. Not knowing where she might be, I made my ears radar antennae, seeking out her exact location. As I washed the dishes, my back became tense with fear. My hands shook, and I couldn't concentrate on my chores. Finally I heard Mother come out of her bedroom and walk down the hall toward the kitchen. For a fleeting moment I looked out the window. I could hear the laughter and screams of the children playing there. For a moment I imagined I was one of them. I smiled.

My imaginary world soon dissolved when I felt Mother breathing down my neck. Startled, I dropped a dish, but before it could hit the floor, I snatched it out of the air. "You're a quick little boy, aren't you?" she sneered. "You can run fast and find time to beg for food along the way. We'll see just how fast you really are." I expected her to bash me, and I tensed my body waiting for her to strike. When it didn't happen, I expected her to leave and return to her TV show, but that didn't happen either. She remained behind me watching my every move. I could see her reflection in the kitchen window. She saw this, and the reflection smiled back at me in the window. It was a frightening smile and an eerie experience, much like a horror movie.

When I finished the dishes, I began cleaning the bathroom. Mother sat on the toilet as I cleaned the bathtub. When I was on my hands and knees scrubbing the tile floor, she calmly and quietly stood behind me. I expected her to come around and kick me in the face, but she didn't. As I continued my chores, my anxiety grew as I wondered what she had in mind for me. I knew she was going to beat me, but I didn't know when or where. It seemed to take forever for me to finish the bathroom. By the time I did, my legs and arms were shaking with anticipation. I couldn't concentrate on anything but her. Whenever I found the courage to look up at her, she smiled and said, "Faster young man. You'll have to move much faster than that."

By dinner time I was exhausted with fear and with not knowing what was going to happen to me. I almost fell asleep as I waited for Mother to call me to clear the table and wash the evening dishes. Standing alone downstairs in the garage, my insides became unglued. I so badly wanted to run upstairs and urinate in the toilet, but I knew that without her permission to move, I was a prisoner. "Maybe that is what she has planned for me," I told myself. "Maybe she wants me to drink my own pee." At first the thought was too crude to imagine, but I knew I had to be prepared to deal with anything she might throw my way. The more I tried to think of the many things she might do to me, the more my inner strength seemed to wash away. Then an idea flashed in my brain. I now knew why Mother had followed every step I took. She wanted to maintain a constant pressure on me by leaving me unsure of when or where she would strike. Before I could think of a counter plan, Mother bellowed for me to come upstairs. In the kitchen she told me that only the speed of lightening would save me and I had better wash the dishes in record time. "Of course," she said, "there is no need to tell you that you are going without dinner tonight, but not to worry, I have a cure for your hunger."

A couple of hours later, after I had finished the evening chores, Mother told me to wait downstairs. I stood with my back against the hard wall, wondering what plans she had for me. I had no idea. I broke out in a cold sweat that seemed to seep through to my bones. I was so tired, and while standing there I went to sleep. When I felt my head roll forward, I snapped it upright, waking myself. No matter how hard I tried to stay awake, I couldn't control my head, and it bobbed up and down like a cork in water. While in this trance-like state, I could feel the strain lift my soul away from my body as if I were floating. I felt as light as a feather until my head rolled forward again, jolting me awake. I was too afraid to fall into a deep slumber. I stared through the molded garage window, hearing the sounds of cars driving by and watching the red flashes of planes flying overhead. I wished with all my heart that I could fly away.

Hours later after Ron and Stan went to bed, Mother ordered me to return upstairs. I dreaded every step, for I knew the time had come. She had drained me emotionally and physically. I didn't know what she had planned, but I was at a point where I actually wished that she would beat me and get it over with.

As I opened the door, a calmness enveloped me. The house was dark except for the kitchen light in front of me. I could see Mother sitting by the breakfast table. I stood stoically facing her. She smiled, and I could tell by her slumped shoulders that booze had her in deep six. In a strange way I knew she wasn't going to beat me. My thoughts became cloudy, but my trance broke when she got up and strolled over to the kitchen sink. She knelt down, opened the sink cabinet and removed a bottle of ammonia. I became dumbstruck, still unable to figure out her plan. She got a tablespoon and poured some ammonia into the spoon. My brain was too rattled to think. As much as I wanted to, I could not get my numbed brain into gear.

With the spoon in her hand, Mother began to creep toward me. Some of the ammonia sloshed from the spoon, spilling onto the floor. I almost laughed inside. "That's all? That's it? All she is going to do is have me swallow some of this?" I said to myself.

By instinct I backed away from her until my head struck the counter top by the stove. For some reason I wasn't afraid. I was so tired. All I could think of was, "Come on, let's go. Let's get it over with." As Mother bent down, she again told me that only speed would save me. I tried to understand her puzzle, but my mind was too cloudy.

Without hesitation I opened my mouth, and she rammed the cold spoon deep into my throat. Again I told myself that this was too easy, but only a moment later, I couldn't breathe. I stood wobbling in front of Mother, feeling as if my eyes were going to pop through my skull. I fell on the floor on my hands and knees. "Bubble!" my brain screamed. I pounded the kitchen floor with all my strength trying to swallow, trying to concentrate on the bubble of air stuck in my esophagus. Tears of fear streamed down my cheeks. After a few seconds I could feel the force of my pounding fists weaken. My fingernails scraped the floor. My eyes became fixed on the floor where the colors seemed to run together. I began to feel weak, and I thought I was going to die.

I am not sure, but I think I fainted. When I came to my senses, I could feel Mother slapping me on the back. The force of her blows made me burp, and I was again able to breathe. As I forced huge gulps of air back into my lungs, Mother returned to her glass of booze. She took a deep drink, looked down at me and blew a mist of air in my direction. "Now that wasn't so hard, was it?" she said, finishing her glass before dismissing me downstairs to my cot.

The next evening was a repeat performance, but this time in front of Father. She boasted to him, "This will teach the boy to quit stealing food!" I knew she was only doing it for her sick, perverted pleasure. Father watched as Mother gave me another dose of ammonia. But this time it was much more difficult for her. She had to pry my mouth open, and by thrashing my head from side to side, I was able to make her spill most of the cleaner onto the floor. I got enough though, to get the same effect as the night before. Again I clenched my fingers together beating the floor. I looked up at Father, trying to call out to him. My thoughts were clear, but no sound came through my mouth. He simply stood there, showing no emotion as I then stared at his feet. As if she were kneeling to pet one of her dogs, Mother again slapped me on the back a few times before I blacked out.

The next morning while cleaning the bathroom, I looked in the mirror to inspect my sore tongue. Layers of flesh were scraped away while remaining parts were raw and red. I stood staring into the sink feeling how lucky I was to be alive. I truly felt that I was close to death both nights.

Although she never made me swallow ammonia again, she did make me drink spoonfuls of Clorox a few times. But her favorite seemed to be dishwashing soap. Using the cap, she squeezed the cheap, pink liquid down my throat and sent me to stand in the garage. My mouth became so dry, I sneaked away to the garage faucet and filled my stomach full of the water I so strongly craved. Soon I discovered my dreadful mistake and diarrhea took hold. I cried out to Mother upstairs, begging her to let me use the toilet upstairs. She refused. I stood downstairs afraid to move as clumps of the watery fecal matter fell through my underwear and down my pant legs onto the floor.

I felt so degraded I cried like a baby. I had no self respect, no self worth of any kind. I needed to go to the bathroom again, but I was too afraid to move. Finally, as my bowels twisted and turned painfully, I gathered the last of my dignity. I waddled to the garage sink, grabbed a five-gallon bucket and squatted to relieve myself. I closed my eyes trying to think of a way to clean myself and my clothes when the garage door opened behind me. I turned my head to see Father, looking on dispassionately as his son "mooned" him and the brown seepage spilled into the bucket. I was lower than a dog doing his job on somebody else's lawn.

Mother didn't always win. Once during a week when I was not allowed to attend school, she squeezed the soap into my mouth and told me to clean the kitchen. She didn't know it but I didn't swallow the soap. As the minutes passed, my mouth became filled with a combination of soap and saliva. I simply refused to swallow. When I finished the kitchen chores, I raced downstairs to empty the trash. I smiled from ear to ear as I closed the door behind me and spit out the mouthful of diluted pink soap. When I reached the trash cans by the garage door, I reached into the smaller one and plucked out a used paper towel and wiped out the inside of my mouth to ensure that I removed every speck of soap. After I finished, I felt as though I had won the Olympic Marathon. I was proud of myself for beating her at her own game.

Even though Mother caught me in most of my attempts to steal food, she didn't catch me all the time. After months of being confined for hours at a time in the garage, my courage built up until I was able to steal bits of frozen food from the freezer there. I was fully aware that I could pay for my crime at any time, so I ate every morsel as if it were my last meal.

In the darkness of the garage I closed my eyes, dreaming I was a king dressed in the finest robes eating the best food mankind had to offer. I never knew when my next meal would come, and for the most part I didn't care. As I held a piece of frozen pumpkin pie crust or a bit of taco, they became fancy hors d'oeuvres in my hands. I was the king, and like a king on his throne, I gazed down on my food and smiled.

Chapter 5

The Accident

The summer of '71 set the tone for the remainder of the time that I lived with Mother.

I had not yet reached my eleventh birthday. For the most part I knew what forms of punishment to expect. To exceed one of her time limits on any of my multiple chores meant no food. If I looked at her or one of my brothers without her permission, I received a slap in the face. If I was caught stealing food, I knew Mother would either repeat an old form of punishment or dream up something new and hideous. Most of the time Mother seemed to know exactly what she was doing, and I could anticipate what she might do next. However, I always kept my guard up and tensed my entire body if I thought she might come my way. It mattered little what her mood might be.

As June turned to early July my morale dwindled. Food was little more than a fantasy. Now I rarely received even left-over breakfast no matter how hard I worked to get it, and I was never fed lunch. As for dinner, I averaged about one evening meal every three days.

One particular early July day began like any other mundane day in my now slave-like existence. I had not eaten in three days. Because school was out for the summer, my options for finding food had diminished greatly. As always during dinner I sat at the bottom of the stairs with my buttocks on top of my hands, listening to the sounds of the family eating. Mother now demanded that I sit on my hands with my head thrust backward in a "prisoner of war" position. I let my head fall forward, half dreaming that I was with them. I must have fallen asleep because I was suddenly awakened by Mother's snarling voice, "Get up here! Move your ass!" she yelled.

At the first syllable of her order I snapped my head level, stood up quickly and sprinted up the stairs. I was hoping and praying that tonight I would get something to soothe my hunger.

I had begun clearing the dishes from the dining room table at a feverish pace when Mother called me into the kitchen. I bowed my head as she began to babble her time limits to me. "You have twenty minutes! One minute, one second more and you go hungry again! Is that understood?"

"Yes, ma'am."

"Look at me when I'm, talking to you!" she snapped.

Obeying her command, I slowly raised my head. As I my head came up, I saw Russell rocking back and forth on Mother's left leg. The harsh tone of Mother's voice didn't seem to bother him. He simply stared at me through a set of cold eyes. Even though Russell was only four or five years old at the time, he had become Mother's "Little Nazi," watching my every move, making sure I didn't steal any food. Sometimes he would make up tales for Mother so he could watch me receive punishment. It wasn't really Russell's fault. I knew Mother had brainwashed him, but I had begun to turn cold toward him and hate him just the same.

"Do you hear me?" Mother yelled. "Look at me when I am talking to you!" As I looked at her, Mother snatched a carving knife from the counter top by the kitchen stove and screamed, "If you don't finish on time, I am going to kill you!"

Her words had no effect on me. She had said the same thing over and over again for almost a week now. Even Russell wasn't fazed by her threat. He kept on rocking on Mother's leg as if he were riding a stick pony. She apparently wasn't pleased with her renewed scare tactic because she continued to badger on and on as the clock ticked away on my time limit. I was wishing she would shut up and let me work. I wanted to meet her time limits. I wanted so much to have something to eat. I dreaded so much going to sleep another night.....

Suddenly something looked very wrong! I tried to focus my

eyes on Mother. She had begun to wave the knife in her right hand. Again I was not overly frightened. She had done this before too. "Eyes," I told myself. "Look at her eyes." I did, and they seemed normal for her, half glazed over. But my instincts told me there was something wrong. Something very wrong. I didn't think she was going to hit me, but my body began to tense anyway. As I became more tense, I saw what was wrong. Partly because of Russell's rocking motion and partly because of the motion of her arm and hand with the knife, her whole body began to weave back and forth. For a moment I thought she was going to fall.

She tried to regain her balance, snapping at Russell to let go of her leg. At the same time she continued to berate me. By then her upper body looked like a rocking chair that was rocking out of control. Forgetting about her useless threats, I began to imagine that the old drunk was going to fall flat on her face. I focused all of my attention on her face. Out of the corner of my eye I saw a blurred object fly from her hand. A sharp pain erupted from just above my stomach. I tried to remain standing, but my legs gave out and I blacked out.

As I regained consciousness, I felt a warm sensation below my chest as though something was flowing out. It took me a few seconds to realize where I was. I sat propped up on the toilet. I turned toward Russell who began chanting, "David's going to die. David the bad boy is going to die." I moved my eyes toward my stomach. On her knees Mother was hastily applying a thick wad of gauze to a place on my stomach where dark red blood was pumping out. I tried to say something. I knew it was an accident. I wanted Mother to know that I forgave her, but I felt too faint to speak. My head slumped forward again and again as I tried to hold it up. I lost track of time as I returned to darkness.

When I awakened again, Mother was still on her knees wrapping a cloth around my lower chest. She knew exactly what she was doing. Many times when we were younger, Mother told Ron, Stan and me how she had intended to become a nurse until she met Father. Whenever she was confronted with an accident around the home, she was in complete control. I never doubted her nursing abilities for a second. I waited for her to load me in the car and take me to the hospital. I felt sure that she would. It was just a matter of time. I felt a curious sense of relief. I felt in my heart that it was over. This whole charade of living like a slave would now surely come to an end. Even Mother could not lie about this one. I felt that I was somehow free.

It took Mother nearly half an hour to dress my wound. There was no remorse in her eyes. I thought that at the very least she would try to comfort me with her soothing voice. Looking at me with no emotion, she stood up, washed her hands and told me I now had thirty minutes to finish the dishes. I shook my head, trying to understand what she had said. After a few seconds I knew what she was doing. Just as she had in the arm incident a few years ago, Mother was not going to acknowledge what had happened.

I had no time for self pity. The clock was running. I stood up, wobbled for a few seconds, then made my way to the kitchen. With every step, pain ripped through my ribs and blood seeped through my ragged T-shirt. By the time I reached the kitchen sink, I leaned over and panted like an old dog.

From the kitchen I could hear Father in the living room, flipping through his newspaper. I took a painfully deep breath, hoping that I could shove off and make my way to Dad. But I breathed too hard and fell to the floor. After that I realized that I had to take short, choppy breaths. I made my way into the living room. Sitting on the far end of the couch was my hero. I knew he would take care of Mother and drive me to the hospital. I stood before Father, waiting for him to turn his page and see me. When he did, I said, "Father, Mother stabbed me."

He didn't even raise an eyebrow. "Why?" he asked.

"She threatened to stab me if I didn't do the dishes on time," I answered.

Without even looking at my condition, he returned to his paper. "Well, you had better do what your mother wants," he said.

I stood before Father horrified. I had felt in my heart that he would scoop me up in his arms and take me away. I even imagined him ripping off his shirt to expose his true identity and flying through the air like Superman, knocking Mother aside in his wake.

I turned away. All my respect for Father gone. The savior I had imagined for so long was a phony. I felt more angry at him than I did at Mother. I wished that somehow I could fly away, but the throbbing pain brought me back to reality.

I washed the dishes as fast as my body would let me. I quickly learned that moving my forearm resulted in a sharp pain above my stomach. If I side-stepped from the wash basin to the rinse basin, another pain raced through my body. I could feel what little strength I had draining away. I could not work fast without a great deal of pain. As Mother's time limit passed, so did my chances of getting fed.

I wanted to just lie down and quit, but a stronger urge kept me going. I wanted to show the "bitch" that she could beat me only if I died, and I was determined not to give in, even to death. As I washed the dishes, I discovered that by standing on my toes and leaning my upper body toward the counter top, I could relieve most of the pressure on my lower chest. Instead of side-stepping every few seconds, I washed a few dishes at a time then moved over and rinsed them all at the same time. After drying the dishes, I dreaded the task of putting them away. The cupboards were above my head, and I knew reaching for them would cause great pain. Holding a small plate, I stretched my legs as far as I could and tried to raise my arms above my head to put the dish away. I almost made it, but the pain was too great. I crumbled to the floor.

By now my shirt was saturated with blood. As I tried to regain my feet, I felt Father's strong hands helping me. I angrily brushed him away. "Give me the dish," he said, "I'll put them away. You had better go downstairs and change that shirt." I didn't say a word as I turned away. I looked at the clock. It had taken me nearly an hour and a half to complete my chore. My right hand clamped tightly onto the railing as I slowly made my way downstairs. I could actually see the blood ooze onto my shirt with every step I took.

Mother met me at the bottom of the stairs. As she tore the shirt from my body, I could see that she was doing it as gently as she could. However, she gave me no other comfort. I could see that it was just a matter of business to her. In the past I had seen her treat animals with more compassion than she gave me.

I was so weak that I accidentally fell against her as she was dressing me in an old oversize T-shirt. I expected her to hit me, but she let me rest against her for a few seconds. She then set me at the bottom of the stairs and left. She returned in a few minutes with a glass of water for me to drink. I gulped it down as fast as I could swallow. When I finished the water, Mother told me that she couldn't feed me right away. She said she would feed me in a few hours when I felt better. Again her voice was a monotone, completely without emotion.

Looking outside, I could see the California twilight being overtaken by darkness. Mother told me I could play outside with the boys on the driveway in front of the garage door. My head was not clear. It took me a few seconds to understand what she had said. "Go. Go on," she persisted. With her help I limped out of the garage to the driveway. My brothers casually looked me over, but they were much more interested in lighting and playing with some Fourth-of-July sparklers. As the minutes passed, Mother became more compassionate toward me. She held me by the shoulders as we watched my brothers make figure eights with their sparklers. "Would you like one?" she asked. I nodded yes. She held my hand as she knelt down to light the sparkler. For a moment I imagined the scent of the perfume she used years ago. But she had not used perfume or worn make-up for a long time.

As I played with my brothers, I couldn't help but think about Mother and the change in the way she was treating me. "Is she trying to make up with me?" I wondered. "Is my abusive treatment finally over? Am I back in the family fold?" For a few minutes I didn't care. My brothers seemed to accept my presence, and I felt a feeling of friendship and warmth with them that I thought had been buried forever.

Within a few seconds my sparkler fizzled out. I turned toward the retreating sun. It had been months since I had watched a sunset. I closed my eyes, trying to soak up as much heat as I could. For a few fleeting moments my pain, my hunger, my miserable way of life disappeared. I felt so warm, so alive. I opened my eyes, hoping to capture the moment for the rest of eternity.

Before she went to bed, Mother gave me more water and fed me some small bites of food. I felt like a disabled animal being nourished back to health, but I didn't care.

Downstairs in the garage I lay on my back on an old army-surplus cot. I tried not to think of the pain, but it was impossible to ignore as it crept throughout my body. Finally exhaustion took over my body and my mind, and I drifted off to an uneasy sleep. During the night I had several nightmares. I startled myself, waking up in a cold sweat. Behind me I heard a sound that scared me again. It was Mother. She bent down and applied a cold wash cloth to my forehead. She told me that I had been running a fever during the night. I was too tired and weak to respond. All I could think about was the pain. Later Mother returned to my brothers' downstairs bedroom, which was closer to the garage. I felt safer knowing she was nearby to watch over me.

Soon I drifted back into darkness, and with the fitful sleep came a dreadful dream of sheets of red, hot rain. In the dream I seemed to drench in it. I tried wiping the blood off my body only to find it quickly covered again. When I awoke in the morning, I stared at my hands which were covered with crusted dried blood. The shirt covering my chest was entirely red. I could feel the dried blood on parts of my face. I heard the bedroom door behind me open, and I turned to see Mother walking toward me. I expected more sympathy like she had given me the night before, but it was an empty hope. She gave me none. In a cold voice she told me to clean myself up and begin my chores. As I heard her march up the stairs, I knew nothing had changed. I was still the bastard of the family.

About three days after the "accident" I continued to feel feverish. I didn't dare ask Mother for any aspirin, especially since Father was away at work. I knew she was back to her normal self. I thought the fever was due to my injury. The slit in my stomach had opened up more than once since that night. Quietly, so Mother wouldn't hear me, I crept to the garage sink. I picked up the cleanest rag I could find in my heap of rags. I cracked the water faucet open just enough to let a few drops of water spill onto the rag. I sat down and rolled up my red, soggy shirt. I touched my wound, flinching from the pain. I took a deep breath and as gently as possible pinched the slit. The pain was so bad I threw my head back against the cold concrete floor almost knocking myself out. When I looked at my stomach again, I saw a yellowish-white substance begin to ooze from the red, angry slash. I didn't know much about such things, but I knew it was infected. I started to get up to go upstairs and ask Mother to clean me up. When I was half standing,

I stopped. "No!" I told myself. "I don't need that bitch's help." I knew enough from basic first-aid training to clean a wound, and I began to feel confident that I could do it alone. I wanted to be in charge of myself. I didn't want to rely on Mother or give her any more control over me than she already had.

I wet the rag again and brought it down toward my wound. I hesitated before I touched it. My hands were shaking with fear as tears streamed down my face. I felt like a baby and hated it. Finally I told myself, "You cry, you die. Now take care of the wound." I think I realized in a child's way that my injury probably wasn't life-threatening. So I brainwashed myself to do what I had to do to block out the pain.

I moved quickly before my motivation slipped away. I snatched another rag, rolled it up and stuffed it into my mouth. I focused all my attention on the thumb and first finger of my left hand as I pinched the skin around my slit. With my other hand I wiped away the pus. I repeated the process until blood seeped through, and I was wiping away blood only. Most of the white stuff was gone. The pain from the pinching and wiping was nearly more than I could stand. With my teeth clamped tightly on the rag, my screaming was muffled. I felt as though I was hanging from a cliff. By the time I finished, a river of tears soaked the neck of my shirt. I couldn't see myself, but I must have looked like a monster.

Fearing Mother would catch me not sitting at the bottom of the stairs, I cleaned up my mess then half walked and half crawled to my assigned place at the foot of the staircase. Before I sat on my hands in what I now called my "prisoner of war" position that she demanded, I checked my shirt. Only small drops of blood escaped from the wound to the rag bandage. I willed the wound to heal. Somehow I knew it would. I felt proud of myself. I imagined myself like a character in a comic book who overcame great odds and survived. Soon my head slumped forward and I fell asleep. In my dream I flew through the air in vivid colors. I wore a cape of red. I was Superman.

Chapter 6

While Father Is Away

A fter the knife incident Father spent less and less time at home and more at work. He made excuses to the family, but I didn't believe him. I often shivered with fear as I sat in the garage hoping that for some reason he might not leave. In spite of all that had happened, I still felt he was my protector. When he was home, Mother did only about half the things to me that she did when he was gone.

When Father was home, it became his habit to help me with the evening dishes. Father washed and I dried. While we worked, we talked softly so neither Mother nor the other boys could hear us. Sometimes several minutes would pass without us talking. We wanted to make sure the coast was clear.

Father nearly always broke the ice. "How you doing, Tiger?" he would say.

Hearing the old name that Father used when I was a little boy always brought a smile to my face. "I'm OK," I would answer.

"Did you have anything to eat today?" he often asked. I usually shook my head in a negative gesture.

"Don't worry," he'd say. "Some day you and I will both get out of this mad house."

I knew Father hated living at home, and I felt that it was all my fault. I told him that I would be good and that I wouldn't steal any more food. I told him that I would try harder and do a better job on my chores. When I said these things, he always smiled and assured me that it wasn't my fault.

Sometimes as I dried the dishes, I felt a new ray of hope. I knew Father probably wouldn't do anything against Mother, but when I stood beside him I felt safe.

Like all good things that happened to me, Mother put an end to Father helping me with the dishes. She insisted that "the boy" needed no help. She said that Father paid too much attention to me and not enough to others in the family. Without a fight Father gave up. Mother then had complete control over everybody in the household.

After a while Father didn't even stay home on his days off. He would come in for only a few minutes. After seeing my brothers, he would find me wherever I was doing my chores and say a few sentences and leave. It took him no more than ten minutes to get in and out of the house and be on his way back to his solitude, which he usually found in a bar. When he did talk to me, he'd tell me that he was making plans for the two of us to leave. This always made me smile, but deep inside I knew it was a fantasy.

One day he bent down to tell me how sorry he was. I looked into his face. The change in him frightened me. He had dark black circles around his eyes, and his face and neck were a dark red. His once rigid shoulders were now slumped over. Gray had begun to take over his jet-black hair. Before he left that day, I threw my arms around his waist. I didn't know when I would see him again.

After finishing my chores that day, I rushed downstairs. I had been ordered to wash my ragged clothes and another heap of smelly rags. But that day Father's leaving had left me so sad that I buried myself in the pile of rags and cried. I cried for him to come back and take me away. After a few minutes of self comfort, I settled down and began scrubbing my "Swiss cheese" clothes. I scrubbed until my knuckles bled. I no longer cared about my existence. Mother's house had become unbearable. I wished I could somehow manage to escape the place I now called the "Mad House."

During one period of time when Father was away, Mother starved me for about ten consecutive days. No matter how hard I tried to meet her time limits, I couldn't make it. And the consequence was no food. Mother was completely thorough in making sure I was unable to steal any food. She cleared the dinner table herself, putting the food down the garbage disposal. She rummaged through the garbage can every day before I emptied it downstairs. She locked the freezer in the garage with her key and kept it. I was used to going without food for periods up to three days, but this extended time was terrible. Water was my only means of survival. When I filled the metal ice cube trays for the refrigerator, I tipped the corner of the tray to my mouth. Downstairs I crept to the wash basin and cracked the faucet tap open. Praying that the pipe would not vibrate, I sucked the cold metal until my stomach was so full I thought it would burst.

By the sixth day I was so weak when I awoke on my cot downstairs that I could hardly get up. I worked at my chores at a snail's pace. I felt so tired. My thought responses became unclear. It seemed to take minutes for me to understand each sentence Mother yelled at me. As I slowly pulled my head up to look at her, I could tell that to her it was a game, and a game which she thoroughly enjoyed.

"Oh, poor little baby," she said sarcastically. Then she asked me how I felt and laughed at me when I begged for food. At the end of the sixth day and those that followed, I hoped with all my heart that she would feed me something, anything. I was at a point that I didn't care what it was.

One evening toward the end of her "game" after I had finished my chores, Mother slammed a plate of food in front of me. The cold leftovers were a feast to my eyes. But I was wary; it seemed too good to be true. "Two minutes!" Mother barked. "You have two minutes to eat. That's all." Like lightening I picked up the fork, but the moment before the food touched my mouth, Mother snatched the plate away from me and emptied the food down the garbage disposal. "Too late!" she sneered.

I stood before her dumbstruck. I didn't know what to do or what to say. All I could think of was a question, "Why?" I couldn't understand why she treated me worse than one would treat a criminal. I was so close to the food. I could smell every morsel. I knew she wanted me to cry, but I stood fast and held back the tears.

Alone in the garage I felt I was losing control of myself. I wanted food. I wanted my father. But more than anything I wanted just one ounce of respect, one little bit of dignity. Sitting there on my hands, I could hear my brothers opening the refrigerator to get their desserts, and I hated it. I looked at myself. My skin had a yellowish tint, and my muscles were thin and stringy. Whenever I heard one of my brothers laugh at a television show, I cursed their names. "Lucky bastards! Why doesn't she take turns and beat up on one them for a change?" I cried to myself as I vented my feelings of hatred.

On about the tenth day I had gone without food I had finished the dinner dishes when Mother repeated her "you have two minutes to eat" game. There were only a few bits of food on the plate. I thought she would snatch the plate away again, so I moved with a purpose. I didn't give her a chance to take it away like she had the past three evenings. I grabbed the plate and quickly swallowed the food without chewing it. Within seconds I finished eating all that was on the plate and licked it clean. "You eat like a pig!" Mother snarled at me. I bowed my head, acting as though I cared. But inside I laughed at her, saying to myself, "Fuck you! Say what you want! I got the food!"

Mother had another favorite trick for me while Father was away. She sent me to clean the bathroom with her usual time limits. But this time she put a bucket filled with a mixture of ammonia and Clorox in the room with me and closed the door. The first time she did this, Mother told me that she had read about it in a newspaper and wanted to try it. Even though I acted as if I were frightened, I really wasn't. I was ignorant about what was going to happen. Only when she closed the door and ordered me not to open it did I begin to worry. Once the door was closed, the air in the room began to change quickly. In the corner of the bathroom I dropped to my hands and knees and looked at the bucket. A fine gray mist was swirling toward the ceiling. As I breathed in the fumes, I collapsed and began spitting up. My throat felt like it was on fire. Within minutes it was raw. The gas from the reaction of the ammonia and Clorox mixture made my eyes water. In my agony I worried about not being able to meet her time limits for cleaning the bathroom.

After a few more minutes I thought I would cough up my insides. I knew that Mother wasn't going to give in and open the door. I had to use my head. I pushed the bucket over close to the door. I did this for two reasons: I wanted the mixture as far away from me as possible, and in case Mother did open the door I wanted her to get a nose full of her own medicine. I curled up in the opposite corner of the bathroom with my cleaning rag over my nose, mouth and eyes. Before covering my face, I wet the rag in the toilet. I didn't dare turn on the water in the sink for fear of Mother hearing it. Breathing through the cloth, I watched the mist make its way closer and closer to the floor. I felt as if I were locked in a gas chamber. Then I thought about the small heating vent on the floor by my feet. I knew it turned on and off every few minutes. I put my face next to the vent and sucked in all the air my lungs would hold. In about half an hour Mother opened the door and told me to empty the mixture in the bucket in the drain in the garage before I smelled up her house. Downstairs I coughed up blood for an hour at a time. Of all Mother's punishments I hated her gas chamber the most.

Toward the end of the summer Mother must have become bored with finding ways to torture me around the house. One day after I had completed all my morning chores, she sent me out to mow lawns. This wasn't an altogether new routine. During the Easter vacation from school the spring before she had sent me out to mow. She set a quota on my earnings and ordered me return the money to her. The quota was impossible for me to meet, so in desperation I stole nine dollars from the piggy bank of a small girl who lived in our neighborhood. Within hours the girl's father was knocking on our door. Of course, Mother returned the money and blamed me. After the man left, she beat me until I was black and blue. I only stole the money to try to meet her quota.

The summer mowing plan turned out no better for me than the one during Easter vacation. Going from door to door, I asked people if they cared to have their lawn mowed. No one did. My clothes and my thin arms must have made me a pathetic sight. Out of sympathy one lady gave me a lunch in a brown bag and sent me on my way. Half a block down the street a couple agreed to have me mow their grass. When I finished, I started to run back to Mother's house, carrying the brown bag with me. I intended to hide it before I turned on her block. I didn't make it. Mother was out cruising in her car, and she pulled over and caught me with the bag. Before Mother screeched the station wagon to a stop, I threw my hands into the air like the criminal I was. I remember wishing that lady luck would be with me just one time.

Mother leaped out of the car, snatched the brown bag in one hand and punched me with the other. She then threw me into the car and drove to the house where the lady had made the lunch for me. The woman wasn't home. Mother was convinced that I had sneaked into the lady's house and prepared my own lunch. I knew that to be in the possession of food was the ultimate crime. Silently, I yelled at myself for not ditching the food earlier.

Once home the usual "ten-rounder" left me sprawled on the floor. Mother then told me to sit outside in the back yard while she took "her sons" to the zoo. The section where she ordered me to sit was covered with rocks about an inch in diameter. I lost circulation in much of my body as I sat there on my hands in my "prisoner of war" position. As I sat there, I began to give up on God. I felt that He must hate me. What other reason could there be for a life like mine? All my efforts for mere survival seemed futile. My attempts to stay one step ahead of Mother were useless. A black shadow was always over me.

Even the sun seemed to avoid me as it hid in a thick cloud cover that drifted overhead. I slumped my shoulders, retreating into the solitude of my dreams. How much time passed I don't know, but later I could hear the distinctive sound of Mother's station wagon returning to the garage. My time sitting on the rocks was over. I wondered what she had planned for me next. I hoped it was not another gas chamber session. From the garage she yelled for me to follow her upstairs. She led me to the bathroom. My heart sank. I felt doomed. I began taking huge breaths of fresh air, knowing that soon I would need it.

To my surprise there was no bucket or bottles in the bathroom. "Am I off the hook?" I asked myself. This looked too easy. I timidly watched Mother as she turned the cold water tap in the bathtub fully open. I thought it was odd that she forgot to turn on the hot water as well. As the tub began to fill with cold water, Mother tore off my clothes and ordered me to get into the tub. I got into the tub and lay down. A cold fear raced throughout my body. "Lower!" Mother yelled. "Put your face in the water like this!" She then bent over and grabbed my neck with both hands and shoved my head under the water. Instinctively I thrashed and kicked, trying desperately to force my head above the water so I could breathe. Her grip was too strong. Under the water I opened my eyes, and I could see bubbles escape my mouth and float to the surface as I tried to shout. I tried to thrust my head from side to side as I saw the bubbles becoming smaller and smaller. I began to feel weak. In a frantic effort I reached up and grabbed her shoulders. My fingers must have dug into her because Mother let go. She looked down on me, trying to get her breath. "Now keep your head below the water, or next time it will be longer!"

I submerged my head, keeping my nostrils barely above the surface of the water. I thought of alligators in a swamp. When Mother left the bathroom, her plan became more clear to me. I was lying stretched out in the tub. The water was unbearably cold. It was as though I was in a refrigerator. I was too frightened of Mother to move, so I kept my head under the surface as ordered.

Hours passed and my skin began to wrinkle. I still felt that I didn't dare touch any part of my body to try to warm it. I did raise my head out of the water far enough to hear better. Whenever I heard somebody walk down the hall outside the bathroom, I quietly slid my head back into the coldness.

Usually the footsteps I heard was one of my brothers going to their bedroom. Sometimes one of them came into the bathroom to use the toilet. They just glared at me, shook their heads and turned away. I tried to imagine I was in some other place, but I could not relax enough to daydream.

Before the family sat down for dinner, Mother came into the bathroom and yelled at me, telling me to get out of the bathtub and put on my clothes. I responded immediately, grabbing a towel to dry myself. "Oh, no!" she screamed. "Put your clothes on the way you are!" Without hesitating, I obeyed her command. My clothes were soaked as I ran downstairs to sit in the back yard as instructed. The sun was beginning to set, but half the yard was still in direct sunlight. I tried to sit in the sunny area, but Mother ordered me to sit in the shade. In the corner of the back yard while sitting in my P.O.W. position, I shivered. I wanted only a few seconds of that warm sunshine, but with every passing minute my chances of getting warm were becoming less and less. From the upstairs window I could hear the sound of the family passing dishes full of food to each other. Once in a while a burst of laughter would come through the window. Since Father was home, I knew that whatever Mother was serving was good. I wanted to turn my head and look up and see them eating, but I didn't dare. I lived in a different world. I didn't even deserve a glance at the good life.

The bathtub and the back yard treatment became routine. At times when I lay in the tub, my brothers brought their friends to the bathroom to look at their naked brother. Their friends often scoffed at me. "What did he do this time?" they'd ask. Most of the time my brothers just shook their heads, saying, "I don't know."

With the start of school in the fall came the hope of a temporary escape from my dreary life. Our fourth grade home room class had a substitute teacher for the first two weeks. They told us that our regular teacher was ill. The substitute teacher was younger than most of the other staff, and she seemed more lenient. At the end of the first week she passed out ice cream to those students whose behavior had been good. I didn't get any the first week, but I tried harder and received my reward at the end of the second week. The new teacher played pop hits on 45-rpm records and sang to the class. We really liked her. When Friday afternoon came, I didn't want to leave. After all the other students had gone, she bent close to me and told me I would have to go home. She knew I was a problem child. I told her that I wanted to stay with her. She held me for a moment then got up and played the song I liked best. After that I left. Since I was late, I ran home as fast as I could and raced through my chores. When I was finished, Mother sent me to the back yard to sit on the cold cement deck.

That Friday I looked up at the thick blanket of fog covering the sun and cried inside. The substitute teacher had been so nice to me. She treated me like a real person, not like some piece of filth lying in the gutter. As I sat outside feeling sorry for myself, I wondered where she was and what she was doing. I didn't understand it at the time, but I had a crush on her.

I knew that I wasn't going to be fed that night or the next. Since Father wasn't home, I would have a bad weekend. Sitting in the cool air in the back yard on the steps, I could hear the sounds of Mother feeding my brothers. I didn't care. Closing my eyes, I could see the smiling face of my new teacher. Her beauty and kindness kept me warm.

By October my morbid life was in full swing. Food was

scarce at school. I was easy prey for school bullies, who beat me up more than once. After school I had to run home and spill the contents of my stomach for Mother's inspection. Sometimes she would have me start my chores right away. Sometimes she would fill the bathtub with water. If she was really in a good mood, she fixed up the gas mixture for me in the bathroom. If she got tired of having me around her house she sent me out to find some mowing jobs, but not before beating me. A few times she whipped me with the dog's chain. It was very painful, but I just gritted my teeth and took it. The worst pain was a blow to the backs of my legs with the broom handle. Sometimes blows from the broom handle would leave me on the floor barely able to move. More than once I hobbled down the street pushing that old wooden lawn mower, trying to get her some money.

There finally came a time when it didn't do me any good for Father to be home because Mother had forbidden him to see me. My hope deteriorated and I began to believe that my life would never change. I thought I would be Mother's slave for as long as I lived. With every passing day my willpower became weaker. I no longer dreamed of Superman or some imaginary hero who would come and rescue me. I knew that Father's promise to take me away was a hoax. I gave up praying and thought only of living my life one day at a time.

One morning at school I was told to report to the school nurse. She questioned me about my clothes and the various bruises that spanned the length of both my arms. At first I told her what Mother had instructed me to tell her. But as my trust in her began to grow, I told her more and more about Mother. She took notes and told me I should come to see her anytime I wanted to talk to somebody. I learned later that the nurse became interested in me because of some reports she had received from the substitute teacher earlier in the school year.

During the last week in October it was tradition at Mother's house for the boys to carve designs on pumpkins. I had been denied this privilege since I was seven or eight years old. When the night came to carve the pumpkins, Mother filled the tub just as soon as I had finished my chores. Again she warned me about keeping my head under the water. As a reminder she grabbed my neck and pushed my head under the water. Then she stormed out of the bathroom, turning the light out as she went. Looking to my left, I could see through the small bathroom window that night was beginning to fall. I passed the time by counting to myself. I started at one and stopped at one thousand. Then I started over. As the hours passed, I could feel the water slowly draining away. As the water drained, my body became colder and colder. I cupped my hands between my legs and laid the length of my body against the right side of the bathtub. I could hear the sounds of Stan's Halloween record that Mother had bought for him several years before. Ghosts and ghouls howled and doors creaked open. After the boys had carved their pumpkins, I could hear Mother in her soothing voice telling them a scary story. The more I heard, the more I hated each and every one of them. It was bad enough waiting like a dog out in the back yard on the rocks while they enjoyed dinner, but having to lie in the cold bathtub shivering to keep warm while they ate popcorn and listened to Mother's story made me want to scream.

Mother's tone of voice that night reminded me of the kind mother I had loved so many years ago. Now even the boys didn't acknowledge my presence in the house or the family. I meant less to them than the spirits that howled from Stan's record. After the boys went to bed, Mother came into the bathroom. She appeared startled to see me still lying in the bathtub. "Are you cold?" she sneered. I shivered and shook my head indicating that I was very cold. "Well, why doesn't my precious little boy get his ass out of the bathtub and warm his hide in his father's bed?"

I stumbled out of the tub, put on my underwear and crawled into Father's bed, soaking the sheets with my wet body. For reasons I didn't understand, Mother had decided to have me sleep in the master bedroom whether Father was home or not. She slept in the upstairs bedroom with my brothers. I didn't really care as long as I didn't have to sleep on the cot in the cold garage. That night Father was home; but before I could say anything to him, I fell asleep.

By Christmas my spirit was drained. I detested being home during the two-week vacation and impatiently awaited my return to school. On Christmas Day I received a pair of roller skates. I was surprised to get anything at all, but as it turned out, the skates were not given in the spirit of Christmas. The skates proved to be just another tool for Mother to get me out of the house and make me suffer. On weekends during the following winter, Mother had me skate outside when the other children were inside because of the cold weather. Up and down the block I skated without even a jacket to keep me warm. I was the only child outside in the neighborhood. More than once Tony, one of our neighbors, stepped outside to get his afternoon newspaper and saw me skating. He'd give me a cheerful smile before hurrying back inside to get away from the cold. In an effort to keep warm, I skated as fast as I could. I could see smoke rising from the chimneys of houses that had fireplaces. I wished that I could be inside sitting by a fire. Mother had me skate for hours at a time. She called me in only when she wanted me to complete some chore for her.

At the end of March that year Mother went into labor while we were home from school on Easter vacation. As Father drove her to a hospital in San Francisco, I prayed that it was the real thing and not false labor. I so badly wanted Mother out of the house. I knew that with her gone, Father would feed me. I was also happy to be free from the beatings.

While Mother was in the hospital, Father let me play with my brothers. I was immediately accepted back into the fold. We played "Star Trek," and Ron gave me the honor of playing the role of Captain Kirk. The first day Father served sandwiches for lunch and let me have seconds. When Father went to the hospital to see Mother, the four of us boys played across the street at the home of a neighbor named Shirley. Shirley was kind to us and treated us as though we were her own children. She kept us entertained with games like ping-pong, or she let us run wild outside. In some ways Shirley reminded me of Mother in the early days before she started beating me.

In a few days Mother came home. She presented the family with a new baby brother named Kevin. After a few weeks had passed, things returned to normal. Father stayed away most of the time, and I continued to be the scapegoat upon which Mother vented her frustrations.

Mother had rarely spent much time with neighbors, so it was uncharacteristic of her when she and Shirley became close friends. They visited each other daily. In Shirley's presence Mother played the role of the loving, caring parent as she had when she was a Cub

Scout den-mother. After several months Shirley asked Mother why David was not allowed to play with the other children. She was also curious why David was punished so often. Mother had a variety of excuses. David either had a cold or he was working on a school project. Eventually she told Shirley that David was a bad boy and deserved being grounded for a long, long time.

In time the relationship between Shirley and Mother became strained. One day for no apparent reason Mother broke all ties with Shirley. Shirley's son was not allowed to play with the boys, and Mother ran around the house calling her a bitch. Even though I wasn't allowed to play with the others, I felt a little safer when Shirley and Mother were friends.

One Sunday during the last month of summer, Mother came into the master bedroom where I had been ordered to sit on my hands in my P.O.W. position. She got me up and had me sit on the corner of the bed. She then told me that she was tired of the life we were living. She told me she was sorry and that she wanted to make up for all the lost time. I smiled from ear to ear as I jumped into her arms and held her tightly. As she ran her hand through my hair, I began to cry. Mother cried too, and I began to feel that my bad times were finished. I let go of our hug and looked into her eyes. I had to know for sure. I had to hear her say it again. "Is it really over?" I asked timidly.

"It's over, sweetheart. After this moment I want you to forget any of it happened at all. You will try to be a good boy, won't you?"

I shook my head.

"Then I'll try to be a good mother."

After our talk Mother let me take a warm bath and put on the new clothes I had received for Christmas. I had not been allowed to wear them before. Mother then took all four of us boys bowling while Father stayed home with Kevin. On the way home from the bowling alley, Mother stopped to shop at a grocery store and bought each of us a toy top. When we got home, Mother said I could play outside with the other boys, but I took the top to the corner of the master bedroom and played by myself. For the first time in years, with the exception of holidays when we had guests in the house, I ate with my family at the dinner table. Things were happening too fast, and I felt that somehow it was too good to be true. As happy as I was, I felt as though I were walking on eggs. I thought for sure Mother would wake up and change back to her old self. But she didn't. I ate all I wanted for dinner, and she let me watch television with my brothers before we went to bed. I thought it was strange that she wanted me to continue to sleep with Father, but she said she wanted to be near the baby.

The next day while Father was at work a lady from social services came to our house in the late afternoon. Mother sent me outside to play with my brothers while she talked to the lady. They talked for more than an hour. Before the lady left, Mother called me into the house. The lady wanted to talk to me for a few minutes. She wanted to know if I was happy. I told her I was. She wanted to know if I got along all right with my mother. I told her I did. Finally she asked me if Mother ever beat me. Before answering, I looked up at Mother, who smiled politely. I felt as though a bomb had exploded deep in the pit of my stomach. I thought I would throw up. It had suddenly occurred to me why Mother had changed the day before, why she had begun to be nice to me. I felt like a fool because I had fallen for it. I was so hungry for love I had swallowed the whole charade.

Mother's hand on my shoulder brought me back to reality. "Well, tell her, sweetheart," Mother said, smiling again. "Tell her that I starve you and beat you like a dog," Mother snickered, trying to get the lady to laugh too.

I looked at the lady. My face felt flushed, and I could feel the beads of sweat forming on my forehead. I didn't have the guts to tell the lady the truth. "No, it's not like that at all," I said. "Mom treats me pretty good."

"And she never beats you?" the lady asked.

"No..uh...., I mean only when I get punished....when I'm a bad boy," I said, trying to cover up the truth. I could tell by the look Mother gave me that I had said the wrong thing. She had brainwashed me for years, and I had said it badly. I could also tell that the lady had picked up on the communication between me and Mother.

"All right," the lady said. "I just wanted to stop in and say hello." After exchanging pleasantries, Mother walked her visitor to the door.

When the lady was clearly gone, Mother closed the door in a rage. "You little shit!" she screamed. I instinctively covered my face when she began swinging. She hit me several times then banished me to the garage. After she had fed my brothers, she called me up to do my evening chores. As I washed the dishes, I didn't feel all that bad. Deep in my heart I had known she was being nice to me for some reason other than loving me. I should have known she didn't mean it because she acted the same way when somebody like Grandma came over for the holidays. At least I had enjoyed two good days. I hadn't had two good days for a long time, so in an odd way it was worth it. I settled back into my routine and relied on my solitude to keep me going. At least I didn't have to walk on eggs any more wondering when the roof was going to fall in on me. Things were back to normal, and I was again the servant for the family.

Even though I had begun to accept my fate, I never felt as alone as I did on the mornings that Father went to work. He got out of bed on work days about five a.m. He didn't know it, but I was always awake too. I'd listen to him shaving in the bathroom, and I would hear him walking to the kitchen to get something to eat. I knew that when he put on his shoes, he was about ready to leave the house. Sometimes I turned over just in time to see him pick up his dark blue Pan Am overnight bag. He'd kiss me on the forehead and say, "Try to make her happy and stay out of her way."

I tried not to, but I always cried. I didn't want him to leave. I never told him, but I am sure he knew. After he closed the front door, I counted the steps that it took him to get to the driveway. I heard him walking on the pathway that led away from our house. The rest was left to my imagination. In my mind I could see him turning left down the block to catch the bus to San Francisco. Sometimes when I was brave, I hopped out of bed and ran to the window so I could catch a glimpse of him. Usually I stayed in bed and rolled over to the warm place where he had slept. I imagined that I could hear him long after he was gone. And when I accepted the fact that he was gone, I had a cold, hollow feeling deep in my soul. I loved Father so much. I wanted to be with him forever, and I cried inside because I never knew when I was going to see him again.

Chapter 7
The Lord's Prayer

A bout a month before I entered the fifth grade, I came to believe that for me, there was no God.

As I sat alone in the garage or read to myself in the near darkness of my parents' bedroom, I came to realize that I would live like this for the remainder of my life. No just God would leave me like this. I believed that I was alone in my struggle and that my battle was one of survival.

By the time I had decided that there was no God who was going to help me, I had totally disconnected myself from all physical pain. Whenever Mother struck me, it was as if she were taking out her aggressions on a rag doll. Inside my emotions swirled back and forth between fear and intense anger. But on the outside I was a robot, rarely revealing my emotions and then only when I thought it would please the "bitch" and work to my advantage. I held in my tears, refusing to cry because I didn't want to give her the satisfaction of my defeat.

At night I no longer dreamed, nor did I let my imagination work during the day. The once vibrant escapes of watching myself fly through the clouds in bright blue costumes were a thing of the past. When I fell asleep, my soul became consumed in a black void. I no longer awoke in the mornings refreshed. I awoke tired and told myself that I had one day less to live in this world. I shuffled through my chores, dreading every moment of every day. With no dreams I found that words like hope and faith were only letters randomly put together into something meaningless, words only for fairy tales.

When I was infrequently afforded the luxury of food, I ate like a homeless dog, grunting like an animal at Mother's commands. I no longer cared when she made fun of me as I hurried to devour even the smallest morsel. Nothing was below me. One Saturday while I was washing the morning dishes, Mother scraped some half-eaten pancakes from a plate onto the dogs' dish. Her well-fed pets picked at the food until they wanted no more then walked away to find a place to sleep. Later, as I put away some pots and pans in a lower cabinet, I crawled on my hands and knees to the dogs' dish and ate what was left of the pancakes. As I ate, I could smell traces of the dogs, but I ate anyway. It hardly bothered me. I fully realized that if the "bitch" caught me eating what rightfully belonged to the dogs, I would pay dearly, but getting food any way I could was my only means of existing.

Inside my soul became so cold I hated everything. I despised the sun, for I knew I would never be able to play in its warm presence. I cringed with hate whenever I heard other children laughing as they played outside. My stomach coiled whenever I smelled food about to be served to somebody else, knowing it was not for me. I wanted so much to strike out at something every time I was called upstairs to play the role of the family slave by picking up after those slobs.

I hated Mother most and wished that she were dead. But before I wished her dead, I wanted her to feel the magnitude of my pain and the utter totality of my loneliness for all those years. During all the years when I had prayed to God, He answered me only once. One day when I was five or six years old, Mother had thrashed me from one end of the house to the other. That night before getting into bed, I got down on my knees and prayed to God. I asked Him to make Mother sick so she couldn't hit me any more. I prayed long and hard, concentrating so much that I went to bed with a headache. Much to my surprise, the next morning Mother was sick. She lay on the couch all day, barely moving. Since Father was at work, my brothers and I took care of her as though she were a patient of ours.

As the years passed and the beatings became more intense, I thought about Mother's age and tried to calculate when she might die. I longed for the day when her soul would be taken into the depths of hell, and I would be free of her.

I also hated Father. He was fully aware of the hell I lived in, but he lacked the courage to rescue me as he had promised so many times in the past. But as I examined my relationship with Father, I realized that he considered me part of the problem. I believe he thought of me as a traitor. Many times when the "bitch" and Father had heated arguments Mother involved me. She would yank me from wherever she found me and demand that I repeat every vile word Father might have used in their past arguments. I fully realized what her game was, but having to choose between them was not difficult. Mother's wrath was much worse for me. I always shook my head, timidly saying what she wanted to hear. She would then scream for me to repeat the words to her in Dad's presence. Much of the time she insisted that I make up the words if I couldn't remember. This bothered me a great deal because I knew that in an effort to avoid a beating, I was biting the hand that often fed me. In the beginning I tried to explain to Father why I had lied and turned against him. At first he told me that he understood, but eventually I knew he had lost faith in me. Instead of feeling sorry, I only hated him more.

The boys who lived upstairs were no longer my brothers. Sometimes in years past, they had managed to encourage me a little. But in the summer of '72 they took turns hitting me and appeared to enjoy throwing their weight around. It was obvious that they felt superior to the family slave. When they approached me, my heart became hard as stone, and I am sure they saw the hate in my face. In a rare and empty victory I'd sneer the word "asshole" under my breath as one of them strutted by me. I made sure they didn't hear me. I came to despise the neighbors, my relatives and anybody else who had ever known me and the conditions under which I lived. As I became older and my thought process became more mature, I asked myself how anybody could know me and not have enough charity in their hearts to do something to help me change my life. Hate was all I had left.

At the core of my soul I hated myself more than anybody else or any other thing. I came to believe that everything that happened to me or around me was my own fault because I had let it go on for so long. Hate and jealousy are often close companions. I wanted what others had but saw no way to get it, so I hated them for having it. I wanted to be strong, but inside I knew I was a wimp. I had never had the courage to stand up to the "bitch," so I knew I deserved whatever happened to me. For years Mother had brainwashed me by having me shout aloud, "I hate myself. I hate myself." She was successful. A few weeks before I started the fifth grade, I hated myself so much I wished I were dead.

School no longer held the exciting appeal that it had in prior years. Time spent in the classroom was only a little better than the "hell house" I came from. Time spent outside the classroom was nearly as bad as Mother's home. My classmates had taken over where she left off. I tried to concentrate on the work placed before me, but my pent-up anger often flashed at the wrong time. Once in the middle of class, I stormed out of the room, screaming at everybody as I left. I slammed the door so hard I thought it would shatter the windows. I ran to the rest room and clenched my hands into fists and pounded the tiles. Taunting from my classmates had driven me from the room. One of them was Clifford, a school bully who had caught me more than once running to Mother's house after school. Beating me up was his way of showing off to his friends. All I did was fall to the ground and cover my head. Sometimes Clifford's friends joined the game and took turns kicking me.

Aggie was a tormentor of a different sort. She never failed to come up with new and different ways of telling me how much she wished I would vanish from her life. Her style was absolute snobbery. Aggie made sure she was always the one in charge of a small band of girls. In addition to tormenting me, showing off their fancy clothes seemed to be the main purpose in life for Aggie and her clique. I had always known Aggie didn't like me, but I really didn't learn how much until the last day of school our fourth-grade year. Aggie's mother taught my fourth-grade homeroom, but she was of little help to me. On the last day of school Aggie came into our room acting as though she were vomiting and said, "David 'Smellzer' Pelzer is going to be in my homeroom next year." Her day was not complete until she fired off a rude remark about me to her friends.

I didn't take Aggie very seriously until her rudeness turned to outright cruelty. She actually put me in danger on a fifth-grade field trip to one of San Francisco's Clipper Ships. As I stood alone looking at the water from the bow of the ship, Aggie approached me with an insidious smile and said in a low voice, "Jump!" She startled me, and I looked into her face, trying to understand what she meant. Again she spoke, quietly and calmly, "I said you should go ahead and jump. I know all about you, Pelzer, and jumping is your only way out."

Another voice came from behind her, "She's right, you know." The voice belonged to John, another classmate and one of Aggie's macho buddies. Looking back over the railing, I stared at the cold green water lapping against the wooden side of the ship. For a moment I could visualize myself plunging into the water, knowing I would drown. It was a comforting thought that promised an escape from Aggie, her friends and all that I hated in the world. But my better senses returned and I looked up and fixed my eyes directly on John's eyes and tried to hold my stare. After a few moments he must have felt my anger because he turned away taking Aggie with him.

At the beginning of my fifth-grade year, Mr. Ziegler, my home-room teacher, had no idea why I was such a problem child. Later, after the school nurse had informed him why I had stolen food and why I dressed the way I did, Mr. Ziegler made a special effort to treat me as if I were a normal kid. One of his jobs as sponsor of the school newspaper was to form a committee of kids to find a name for the paper. I came up with a catchy phrase, and a week later my entry was among others in a school-wide election to select the best name for the newspaper. My title won by a considerable margin. Later on during the day the voting took place, Mr. Ziegler took me aside and told me how proud he was that my title had won. I soaked up the praise like water in a sponge. I hadn't been told anything positive for so long I almost cried. At the end of the day after assuring me that I wasn't in trouble, Mr. Ziegler gave me a letter to take to Mother.

Elated, I ran to Mother's house faster than ever before. As I should have expected, my elation was short-lived. The "bitch" tore the letter open, read it quickly and scoffed, "Well, Mr. Ziegler says I should be so proud of you for naming the school newspaper. He also claims that you are one of the top pupils in his class. Well, aren't you special?" Suddenly, her voice turned ice cold and she jabbed her finger at my face and hissed! "Get one thing straight, you little son-of-a-bitch, there is nothing you can do to impress me! Do you understand me? You are a nobody, an 'IT!' You are nonexistent! You are a bastard child! I hate you and I wish you were dead! Dead! Do you hear me? Dead!"

After tearing the letter into tiny pieces, Mother turned away from me and returned to her television show. I stood motionless, gazing at the letter which lay like snowflakes at my feet. Even though I had heard most of the same words over and over again, this time the word "IT" stunned me like never before. She had stripped me of my very identity. In addition to trying to just survive, I had given my all to accomplish something positive. But again I had failed. My heart sank lower than ever before. Her words were no longer coming from the booze; they were words from her heart. I would have been relieved if she had returned with a knife and ended it all. I knelt down, trying to put the many pieces of the letter back together again. It was impossible. I dumped the pieces of the letter in the trash, wishing my life would end. I truly believed at that moment that death would be better than my prospects for any kind of happiness. I was nothing but an "IT."

My morale had become so low that in some self-destructive way I hoped she would kill me, and I felt that eventually she would. In my mind it was just a matter of when she would do it. So I began to purposefully irritate her, hoping I could provoke her enough that she would end my misery. I began doing my chores in a careless manner. I made sure that I forgot to wipe the bathroom floor, hoping that Mother or one of her royal company might slip and fall, hurting themselves on the hard tile floor. When I washed the evening dishes, I left bits of food on the plates. I wanted the "bitch" to know that I didn't care anymore.

As my attitude began to change, I became more and more rebellious. A crisis was reached one day at the grocery store. Mother picked us up after school that day and stopped to shop for groceries. Usually I stayed in the car, but for some reason she decided to take me inside. She ordered me to keep one hand clamped onto the cart and bend my head toward the floor. I deliberately disobeyed her every command. I knew she didn't want a scene in public, so I walked in front of the cart, making sure I was at least an arm's length away from her. If my brothers made any comments to me, I fired back at them, much to their surprise. I simply told myself that I wasn't going to take anybody's shit anymore.

Mother knew that other shoppers were watching us and could hear us, so several times she gently took my arm and told me in a pleasant voice to settle down. It was a good feeling to know that I had the upper hand in the store, but I also knew that once we were outside, I would pay my dues. Just as I thought, she gave me a sound thrashing before we reached the station wagon. As soon as we were in the car, she had me lie on the floor of the back seat so my brothers could take turns stomping me with their feet for "mouthing off" to them and Mother. Immediately after we entered the house, Mother made a batch of ammonia and Clorox and took me to the bathroom. She put the cleaning rag into the solution in the bucket. I think she knew I had been using the rag as a mask. As soon as she slammed the door, I hurried to the heating vent. It didn't come on. No fresh air came through the vent. I must have been in the bathroom for over an hour because the gray fumes filled the small room all the way to the floor. My eyes filled with tears which seemed to activate the poison even more. I spat mucus and heaved until I thought I would faint. When Mother finally opened the door, I bolted for the hallway, but her hand seized me by the neck. She tried to push my face into the bucket, but I fought back and she failed. But failed also was my plan of rebellion. After the longer "gas chamber" incident, I returned to my docile self, but deep inside I could still feel a pressure like a volcano building, waiting to erupt from deep inside my soul.

The only thing that kept me sane was my baby brother Kevin. He was a beautiful baby and I loved him. About three-and-a-half months before he was born, Mother had let me watch a Christmas cartoon special. After the program, for reasons unclear to me, she ordered me to sit in my brothers' room. Minutes later she stormed into the room, wrapped her hands around my neck and began choking me. I twisted my head from side to side, trying to squirm away from her grip. As I began to feel faint, I instinctively kicked her legs, forcing her away from me. I soon regretted the incident.

About a month after Mother's attempt to choke me, she told me that I had kicked her so hard in the stomach that the baby would have a permanent birth defect. I felt like a murderer. Mother didn't stop with just telling me. She had several different versions of the incident for anybody who would listen. She said she had tried to hug me, and I had repeatedly either kicked or punched her in the stomach. She claimed that I had kicked her because I was jealous of the new baby. She said I was afraid the new baby would get more of her attention.

I really loved Kevin, but I didn't have many opportunities to show my love. I do remember one Saturday when Mother took the other boys to a baseball game in Oakland, leaving Father to baby-sit with Kevin while I cleaned the house. After I finished my work, Father let Kevin out of his crib. I enjoyed watching him crawl around in his blue outfit. I thought he was beautiful. When he lifted his head and smiled at me, my heart melted. He made me forget my suffering for awhile. His innocence was hypnotic as I followed him around the house. I wiped the drool from his mouth and stayed one step behind him so he wouldn't get hurt. Before Mother returned, I played a game of patty-cake with him. The sound of Kevin's laughter filled my heart with warmth and later, whenever I felt depressed, I thought of him. I smiled inside when I heard him cry out in joy.

My brief encounter with Kevin quickly faded away and my hatred surfaced again. I tried to bury my feelings, but I couldn't. I knew I was never meant to be loved. I knew I would never live a life like my brothers. Worst of all, I knew that it was only a matter of time until Kevin would hate me as I felt the others did.

Later that fall Mother began directing her frustrations in more directions. She despised me as much as ever, but she began to alienate her friends, her husband, her brother and even her own mother. Even as a small child I knew that Mother didn't get along very well with her family. She felt that everybody was trying to tell her what to do. She never felt at ease with her own mother, who was also a strong-willed person. Grandmother often offered to buy Mother a new dress or take her to the beauty parlor. Her efforts were not successful. Not only did Mother refuse the offers, but she also yelled and screamed until Grandmother left the house. Sometimes Grandmother tried to help me, but that only made things worse. Mother insisted that her appearance and the way she raised her family were "nobody else's damn business." After a few of these confrontations, Grandmother rarely visited Mother's house.

As the holiday season approached, Mother argued more and more with Grandmother on the telephone. She called her own mother every vicious name she could remember. The trouble between Mother and Grandmother was bad for me because after the battle I often became the object of her anger. One time I heard Mother call my brothers into the kitchen and tell them that they no longer had a grandmother or an Uncle Dan.

Mother was equally ruthless in her relationship with Father. When he did come home either to visit or stay for a day, she started screaming at him the moment he came through the door. As a result he often came home drunk. In an effort to stay out of Mother's path, Father often spent his time doing odd jobs outside the house. He even caught her wrath at work. She often telephoned Father at the station and called him names. "Worthless" and "drunken loser" were two of her favorite names for him. After a few calls the fireman who answered the phone would put it down and not page Father. This made Mother furious, and again I became the object of her fury.

For a while Mother banned Father from the house and the only time we saw him was when we drove to San Francisco to pick up his check. One time on our way to get the check, we drove through Golden Gate Park. Even though my anger was ever present, I flashed back to the good times when the park meant so much to the whole family. My brothers were also silent that day as we drove through the park. Everybody seemed to sense that somehow the park had lost its glamour, that things would never be the same again. I think that perhaps my brothers felt the good times were over for them too.

For a short time Mother's attitude toward Father changed. She tried several times to make up with him. She struggled hard to regain lost time, but her time had run out. One Sunday Mother piled everybody into the car and shopped from store to store for a record of German songs. She wanted to create a special mood for Father when he came home. She spent most of that afternoon preparing a feast with the same enthusiasm that had driven her years before. It took her a long time to fix her hair and apply her make-up just right. She even put on a dress that brought back memories of the person she once was. I thought for sure that God had answered my prayers. As she paced around the house straightening anything she thought was out of place, all I could think about was the food. I knew she would find it in her heart to let me eat with the family. It was an empty hope.

Time dragged on and on into the late afternoon. Father was expected to be home by about one in the afternoon, and every time Mother heard an approaching car she dashed to the front door, waiting to greet him with open arms. Sometime after four, Father came staggering in with a friend from work. The festive mood and setting were a surprise to him. From the bedroom I could hear Mother's strained voice as she tried to be extra nice to Father. A few minutes later Father stumbled into the bedroom. I looked up in wonder. I had never seen him so drunk. He didn't need to speak for me to smell the liquor on him. His eyes were beyond the bloodshot stage, and it appeared to be more of a problem than he could manage to stand upright and keep his eyes open. Even before he opened the closet door, I knew what he was going to do. I knew why he had come home. As he stuffed his blue overnight bag, I began to cry inside. I wanted to become smaller and jump into his bag and go with him.

When he finished packing, Father knelt down and mumbled something to me. The longer I looked at him, the weaker my legs felt. My mind was numb with questions. Where is my Hero? What has happened to him? As he opened the door to leave the bedroom, the drunk friend crashed into Father, nearly knocking him down. Father shook his head, and in a sad voice he said, "I can't take it anymore. The whole thing. Your mother, this house, you. I just can't take it anymore." Before he closed the bedroom door I could barely hear him say, "I'm sorry."

That year Thanksgiving dinner was a flop. In some kind of gesture of good faith, Mother allowed me to eat at the table with the family. I sat deep in my chair, quietly concentrating so I wouldn't say or do anything that might upset Mother. I could feel the tension between my parents. They hardly spoke at all, and my brothers chewed their food in silence. Dinner was hardly over when harsh words erupted. After the fight was over, Father left. Mother reached into one of the cabinets for her bottled prize and seated herself at the end of the sofa. She sat alone, pouring glass after glass of alcohol. As I cleared the table and washed the dishes, I could see that this time I wasn't the only one affected by

Mother's behavior. My brothers seemed to be experiencing the same fear I had for so many years.

For a short time Mother and Father tried to be civil to one another. But by Christmas Day they had both become tired of their pretense. The strain of trying to be nice to each other was more than either could bear. As I sat at the top of the stairs while my brothers finished opening their gifts, I could hear angry words being exchanged between them. I prayed that they could somehow make up, if only for that special day. I had a very depressing thought that Christmas morning. I thought that if God had wanted Mother and Father to be happy, then I would have to be dead.

A few days later in early January, Mother packed Father's clothes in boxes and drove with my brothers and me to a place a few blocks from the fire station. There in front of a dingy motel, Father waited. His face seemed to express relief. My heart sank. After years of my useless prayers, I knew it had finally happened; my parents were separating. I closed my fists so tightly I thought my fingers would tear into the palms of my hands. While Mother and the other boys went into Father's motel room, I sat in the car cursing his name over and over. I hated him so much for running out on his family. But perhaps even more, I was jealous of him, for he had escaped and I had not. I still had to live with Mother. Before Mother drove the car away, Father leaned down to the open window where I was sitting and handed me a package. It was some information he had said he would get me for a book report that I was doing at school. I know he was relieved to get away from Mother, but I could also see sadness in his eyes as we pulled away into the downtown traffic.

The drive back to Daly City was solemn. When my brothers spoke, they did so in soft tones that wouldn't upset Mother. When we reached the city limits, Mother tried to humor the boys by treating them at McDonald's. As usual I sat in the car while they went inside. I looked out the open car window at the sky. A dull gray blanket covered everything, and I could feel the cold droplets of fog on my face. As I stared into the fog, I was frightened. There was nothing at all to stop Mother now. What little hope I had was gone. I felt that I no longer had the will to carry on. I felt as if I were a man on death row, not knowing when my time would come.

I wanted to bolt from the car, but I was too scared to even move an inch. For this weakness, I hated myself. Rather than running, I clutched the package Father had given me and smelled it, trying to pick up a scent of Father's cologne.

When I failed to pick up any odor at all I let out a sobbing cry. At that instant I hated God more than anything else in this or any other world. God had known of my struggles for years, but He had stood by watching as things went from bad to worse. He wouldn't even grant me refuge with my own father. God had left me completely cut off from my greatest hope. Inside I cursed his name, wishing I had never been born.

Outside I could hear the sounds of Mother and the boys approaching the car. I quickly wiped my tears and returned to the inner safety of my hardened shell. As Mother drove out of the McDonald's parking lot, she glanced back at me and sneered, "You are all mine now. Too bad your father is not here to protect you." I felt that now all my defenses were useless. I wasn't going to survive. I knew she was going to kill me, if not today, tomorrow. That day I wished she would kill me as quickly as she could.

My brothers wolfed down their hamburgers. Without them knowing it, I clasped my hands together, bent my head down, closed my eyes and prayed again with all my heart. When the station wagon turned onto our drive, I felt that my time had come. Before I opened the car door, I said in a low voice "...and deliver me from evil."

"Amen."

EPILOGUE
Sonoma County, California

I'm so alive.

As I stand facing the beauty of the boundless Pacific Ocean, a late afternoon breeze blows down from the hills behind me. The day is beautiful as the sun makes its final descent and the magic begins. The sky is ready to burn with brilliance as it turns from a soft blue to a bright orange. I stare westward in awe at the hypnotic power of the waves. A giant curl begins to take form then breaks with a thundering crash against the shore. An invisible mist touches my face. The white foamy water covers my feet but quickly surrenders to the power of the surf and moves away. A piece of driftwood has lazily washed ashore at my feet. As I reach to pick it up I see that it is pitted, yet smooth and bleached from its time in the water and the sun. As my fingers reach out, the sea again moves out, dragging the wood with it. For a moment it seems as though the wood is struggling to stay ashore. It leaves a trail behind as it reaches deeper water and bobs violently before giving in to the ocean.

I marvel at the driftwood, thinking how like my former life it is as the turbulent sea pulls it one way and then another. I once promised myself that if I lived through the turbulence, "I would make something of myself." I would be the best person I could be. Today, I am that person, I let go of my past, accepting the fact that the past is only a small part of my life. The black hole is out there, waiting to suck me under and hold me forever. But it is there only if I let it be. I must hold positive control over my life.

The driftwood takes my mind away from the shore and the present. The past comes back. My past has blessed me and made me stronger inside. Once rescued, I adapted quickly. I had learned how to survive a bad situation. I had learned the secret of internal motivation. My experience gave me an outlook others may never know. I learned to appreciate things others take for granted. I made mistakes like anybody else, but I was fortunate enough to bounce back. Instead of dwelling on the past, I maintained the same focus that I taught myself years ago in the garage. I believed that the Lord was over my shoulder, giving me quiet encouragement and strength when I needed it most.

Among my blessings are the opportunities I have had to meet many people who had a positive impact on my life. They are an endless sea of faces, prodding me, teaching me to make the right choices, helping me in my quest for success. They increase my hunger to prevail over my past. Branching out on a different level, I enlisted in the United States Air Force and discovered historical values and an instilled sense of pride and belonging that until then I had never known. After so many years of struggle, my purpose became clear. I learned that America is truly a land where one can come from less than humble beginnings and become a "winner" from within ones self.

The exploding surf brings me back from the past to reality. The piece of driftwood I have been watching disappears in the swirling ocean. With purpose I quickly turn away from the profound spell of the sea and head back to my truck. Minutes later I am racing my Toyota through the snake-like turns, bound for my secret utopia. Years ago when I lived in the dark, I dreamed about my secret place. Now, whenever I can get away, I always return to the river. After stopping to pick up my precious cargo at the Rio Villa in nearby Monte Rio, I'm back on the single lane blacktop. It is a race against time, for the sun is about to set. One of my life-time dreams is about to come true.

As I enter the peaceful city of Guerneville, the 4-Runner truck slows to a snail's pace. I tap the brakes again before turning right on Riverside Drive. With the windows down I fill my lungs with the sweet air from the towering redwoods that gently sway in the evening breeze.

I bring the white Toyota to a stop in front of 17426 Riverside Drive, the same cabin where "the family" stayed on summer vacations a lifetime ago. Like most other things the house has also changed. Two tiny bedrooms have been added behind the fireplace. An attempt was made to enlarge the tiny kitchen before the flood in 1986. The ancient tree stump where my brothers and I played is now in decay. The only thing left untouched are the cabin's darkened cedar ceiling and the river stone fireplace.

I feel sadness as I turn away and lead my wife and son through a small passage next to the cabin that my parents led me and my brothers through years ago. I know the owner; he will not mind our trespassing. In silence the three of us gaze westward. The Russian River is the same as it always was, dark green, smooth as glass as it makes its way every so slowly to the mighty Pacific. Bluejays chide each other as they glide through the air before disappearing into the gigantic redwood trees. The sky is now bathed in streaks of orange and blue. I take a deep breath and close my eyes, savoring the moment as I did years before.

As I open my eyes, a tear rolls down my cheek. I kneel down, wrapping my arms around my son Stephen. Without hesitating, he leans his head back and kisses me. "Love you, Dad."

"I love you, too," I reply.

"And what about me?" my wife Phyllis teases as she embraces me around the shoulders.

I nod my head. "We're all in this together," I answer.

My son looks at the darkening sky. His eyes grow wide as he strains to see the disappearing sun. "Is it always like this?" Stephen asks.

My throat becomes tight. Tears well up again. "This," I answer, spreading my arms outward, "never changes."

Stephen continues to stare at the setting sun, "But aren't changes good, Dad?"

"Sometimes," I reply. "Sometimes."

From above I can hear Phyllis chuckle. Stephen is at that magical age when everything is a question. I glance up at my wife. She knows. She sees my strengths, knows about my struggles, tolerates my shortcomings and my never-ending quest to better myself.

Even now as tears stream down my face, she smiles, letting me have my dignity. She knows why I'm crying. Phyllis knows they are tears of joy.

I'm free.

PERSPECTIVES ON CHILD ABUSE
David Pelzer
Victim

A s a child living in a dark world, I feared for my life and thought I was alone. As an adult I know now that I was not alone. There were thousands of other abused children.

Sources of information vary, but it is estimated that one in five children are physically, emotionally or sexually abused in our country. Unfortunately there are those among the uninformed public who believe that most abuse is nothing more than parents exerting their "right" to discipline their children and letting it get a little out of hand. These same people believe that over-discipline is not likely to follow the child into adulthood. They are tragically misinformed.

On any given day some adult who is the victim of a dark past of child abuse may vent his or her pent-up frustrations on society or on those he or she may love. The public is well informed about the most uncommon cases. Unusual incidents attract the media and boost ratings. We heard about the lawyer father who struck out with his fist and left the child unconscious on the floor and retired to bed. We heard about the father who dunked the small child in the toilet. Both children died. In a more bizarre case both a mother and a father each killed a child and hid their bodies for a period of four years. There are other high profile stories like the abused child who grew into the man who went on a killing spree at a McDonald's, gunning down helpless victims until the police took his life.

More common are the unknowns who disappear, like the

homeless boy who sleeps under a freeway bridge and calls a cardboard box home. Each year thousands of abused girls run away from home and sell their bodies in order to survive. Others strike out by joining gangs who are totally committed to violence and destruction.

Many child abuse victims hide their past deep inside, so deep that the possibility of becoming an abuser themselves is unthinkable. They live normal lives, becoming husbands and wives, raising families and building careers. But the ordinary problems of life often force the former abuse victim to behave as they were taught as children. Spouses and children then become the object of their frustration, and they unknowingly come the full circle, completing the never-ending cycle of rage.

Some child abuse victims stay quietly locked in their shells. They look the other way, believing that by not acknowledging their past it will go away. They seem to believe that above all Pandora's Box must stay closed.

Each year millions of dollars are poured into child protection agencies in our country. These dollars go to local facilities like foster homes and juvenile halls. There are dollar grants to thousands of private organizations whose mission includes basic child abuse prevention, the counseling of abusive parents and the victims. Every year the number grows larger. In 1990 over 2.5 million child abuse cases were reported in the United States. In 1991 the number increased to more than 2.7 million.

Why? What causes the tragedy of child abuse? Is it really as bad as they say? Can it be stopped? And perhaps the most important of all questions, what is abuse like through the eyes of the child?

What you have just read is a story of an ordinary family that was devastated by their hidden secret. The story has two objectives: the first is to inform the reader how a loving, caring parent can change to a cold, abusive monster venting frustrations on a helpless child; the second is the eventual survival and triumph of the human spirit over seemingly insurmountable odds.

Some readers will find the story unreal and disturbing, but child abuse is a disturbing phenomenon that is a reality in our society. Child abuse has a domino effect that spreads to all who touch the family. It takes its greatest toll on the child victim and spreads in the immediate family to the spouse, who is often torn between the child and their mate. From there it goes to other children in the family who do not understand and feel threatened. Also involved are neighbors who hear the screams but do not react, teachers who see the bruises and must deal with a child too distracted to learn, and relatives who want to intervene but do not want to risk relationships.

This is more than a story of survival. It is a story of victory and celebration. Even in its darkest passages, the heart is unconquerable. That the body survives is important, but it is more meaningful that the human spirit prevails.

This is my story and mine alone. For years I was confined to the darkness of my own mind and heart, alone and a pitiful "loser." At first I wanted nothing more than to be like others, but that motivation grew. I wanted to become a "winner." I rejected the shackles of child abuse, and today I am a "winner." For over thirteen years I served my country in the military. I now serve my country giving seminars and workshops to others in need, helping them to break their chains. I bring a message to abused children and those who work with them from one who has been there. I bring a perspective born in the brutal reality of child abuse and nurtured in hope for a better tomorrow. Most important I broke the cycle and became a father whose only guilt is that of spoiling his son with love and encouragement.

Today there are millions in our country in desperate need of help. It is my mission to assist those in need of a helping hand. I believe it is important for people to know that no matter what lies in their past, they can overcome the dark side and press on to a brighter world. It is perhaps a paradox that without the abuse of my past, I might not be what I am today. Because of the darkness in my childhood, I have a deep appreciation for life. I turned tragedy into triumph. This is my story.

Perhaps at no time in the history of our country has the family been under more stress. Economic and social changes have pushed the family to its limit and made child abuse more likely. If society is to come to grips with the problem, it must be exposed. Once exposed, the causes of child abuse can be understood and support can truly begin. Childhood should be carefree, playing in the sun, not living a nightmare in the darkness of the soul.

PERSPECTIVES ON CHILD ABUSE
Steven E. Ziegler
Teacher

S eptember, 1992, began as a typical back-to-school month for
me. In my twenty-second year of teaching, I found the usual
hectic, non-stop confusion. There were close to two-hundred new
students who had names for me to learn and several new faculty
members to welcome aboard. It was good-bye to summer vacation
and hello to additional responsibilities and the annual doom and
gloom from Sacramento regarding money for schools. Nothing had
seemingly changed about the beginning of school until a telephone
message arrived on the twenty-first that rather painfully jolted me
back twenty years: "A David Pelzer would like you to contact his
agent in Omaha, Nebraska, regarding some child abuse reports you
were associated with twenty years ago." The past came back all
too quickly.

Oh, yes, how well I remember David Pelzer. I was a recent
college graduate, a new teacher; and as I look back, I knew little
about the real world of my chosen career. And the thing I knew
least about was child abuse. In the early 70's I didn't know if child
abuse actually existed. If it did, it remained very much in the "closet" as did so many unmentionable lifestyles and behaviors back
then. We have learned so much; yet we have so far to go.

My mind returned to the Thomas Edison School, Daly City,
California, September, 1972. Enter little David Pelzer as one of my
fifth-grade students. I was naive back then, but I was blessed with
a sensitivity that told me there was something terribly wrong in
David's life. Food missing from other students' lunches was traced

to this thin, sad boy. Questionable bruises appeared on exposed parts of his body. Everything began to point to one thing: this kid was being beaten and punished in ways far beyond normal parental practice. It was several years later when I learned that what I was witnessing in my classroom was the third-worst case of child abuse on record in the entire state of California.

It is not for me to tell again all the graphic details my colleagues and I witnessed and reported to the authorities so many years ago. That account remains David's privilege and opportunity in this book. But what a wonderful opportunity it is for this young man to come forward and tell his story so that other children may not suffer. I deeply admire his courage in doing so.

My very best to you, David. There is absolutely no doubt in my mind how far you have truly come.

PERSPECTIVES ON CHILD ABUSE
Valerie Bivens
Social Worker

A s a Social Worker for Child Protective Services in California, I am all too aware of the frequency and severity of crimes against children. This book is the account of one child's unthinkable abuse. We see the child's perception as he moves through a horrifying continuum from an idealistic family life to becoming a "prisoner of war" in his own home. This story is shared with the reader by a survivor, a man of extreme courage and fortitude.

Unfortunately the general public is unaware of the extent of child abuse. These children, victims of outrageous crimes, too often are unable to speak about or against their abusers. Their rage and pain is then turned on themselves or others close to them, and the cycle continues.

We are beginning to hear more about child abuse. Movies and magazine articles on the subject are becoming more frequent, but cases are often sensationalized, and we are too far removed to understand the virtual reality and pain of the victim child. This book enlightens and educates. As we move with David through fear, loss, isolation, pain and rage to eventual hope, the dark world of the abused child becomes painfully clear. We become aware of the child's cry through David Pelzer's eyes, ears and body. We also feel the victim's heart as it moves from unbearable aching to eventual triumph.

PERSPECTIVES ON CHILD ABUSE
Glenn A. Goldberg
*Executive Director of the California Consortium
for the Prevention of Child Abuse*

D avid Pelzer's story must be told so that we can mobilize
Americans to create a country where it won't hurt to be a
child. Millions of our children, our most precious natural resource,
are being victimized by a tragic and unconscionable epidemic of
child abuse and neglect. Both the level and intensity of child mal-
treatment have increased dramatically in the last decade. David's
story will help people understand that our child abuse crisis goes
far beyond excessive spanking. Each year hundreds of thousands
of helpless children are being brutalized and tortured, physically,
emotionally and sexually.

Each act of child abuse reverberates into the future; when a
child gets hurt, we may all suffer the consequences. David Pelzer is
a triumphant survivor of his childhood abuse, and his story is an
inspiration to all of us. We must never forget, however, the tens of
thousands of other children who didn't survive their ordeals and
the millions who are still suffering. The only cure for child abuse is
its prevention, and it is my fervent hope that this book will help
build our growing movement of people working to prevent child
abuse in all its forms.

I NEVER KNEW

I never knew how bad it was;
I heard it did exist.
I was appalled at this crime
That robbed youth
Of their "special" time.

I never knew how bad it hurt;
The bruises and scars aren't seen.
And why somewhere along life's way,
The brutality of abuse
Has made you pay.

I never knew how you felt,
Your self esteem so low.
I only knew you crept away,
And never let your feelings show.

I never knew what I could do;
That I could help somehow.
That all you needed was a friend;
Just someone to be your pal.

But now I know that I can help;
I can make a difference, too.
I'll stand with you; I'll shout with you,
And the rest can't say, "I never knew."

Cindy M. Adams

ABOUT THE AUTHOR

David Pelzer is an affiliate with the nationally recognized speaking, consulting and research firm, **Maun-Lemke, Inc**. He travels throughout the nation giving unique seminars to various groups and corporations. His seminars target motivation, self esteem, goal setting as well as building the will to overcome obstacles. David often works in alcohol and drug awareness programs.

David is involved with child abuse awareness and prevention and foster care programs and various youth at risk associations across the nation. His unique accomplishments have been recognized through a number of awards as well as personal commendations from former Presidents Ronald Reagan and George Bush. In January of 1993, David was honored by the United States Junior Chamber of Commerce as one of The Ten Outstanding Young Americans (TOYA).

David is currently working on the second book of his trilogy entitled **The Lost Boy**. The second book is based on his years in foster care.

David Pelzer lives in Yuba City, California, with his wife Phyllis, his son Stephen and his box turtle named Chuck.

For more information on David Pelzer write **Maun-Lemke, Inc.** at 8031 West Center Road, Suite 222, Omaha, NE 68124, or call 1-800-356-2233.

THE UNITED STATES JUNIOR
CHAMBER OF COMMERCE

Dave is proud to be affiliated with the U.S. Junior Chamber of Commerce (Jaycees). For nearly 75 years, the organization has been providing personal and professional training through civic involvement. The 4,200 chapters nationwide play an important role in shaping and improving their communities.

Key national programming areas include environmental protection (Greenworks!), government awareness, drug and alcohol abuse prevention, firearm safety and farmer education.

The Junior Chamber trains its members to become business, community and government leaders on local to national levels. For more information on the organization that believes 'that service to humanity is the best work in life,' call 1 (800) JAYCEES.

WOULD YOU LIKE TO ORDER
"A CHILD CALLED 'IT'"?

YES! Please send me _____ copies of the book,
"A CHILD CALLED 'IT'" at $7.95 per copy plus $2.05
for postage and handling.

Please send to:

Name _____

Address _____

_____

Telephone (_____) _____

I am enclosing my check in the amount of $ _____.
(Nebraska residents please add 6.5% sales tax)

    or

Please charge to my VISA/MasterCard account.

Account # _____

Expiration Date _____

Signature _____

TO ORDER PLEASE MAIL, FAX OR CALL:
Maun-Lemke, Inc.
8031 West Center Road, Suite 222
Omaha, Nebraska 68124
(800) 356-2233
(402) 391-5540
FAX: (402) 391-1025

For information regarding Mr. Pelzer's presentations
and seminars, please contact **Maun-Lemke** at the above
telephone numbers.